Additional Praise

With spare words and big heart, Meridian Kristi tells a powerful story of learning how to love. Though deeply personal, she also tells many of our stories as she confronts racism, abuse, and societal expectations. With the precision of a poet, her words will expand you.

—Tama Kieves, bestselling author of *A Year Without Fear* and *Thriving Through Uncertainty*

I've always been touched by Meridian's writing. Her stories are poetic, and the poems tell her stories. It is a lyric ride through a love-laden life. Enjoy!

—Terri Tate, author of *A Crooked Smile*

Love in the Rearview Mirror

A Memoir in Stories and Poems

Meridian Kristi

Sidekick Press
Bellingham, Washington

Published 2024
Printed in the United States of America
ISBN: 978-1-958808-35-1
LCCN: 2024908463

Sidekick Press
2950 Newmarket Street, Suite 101-329
Bellingham, Washington 98226
sidekickpress.com

Love in the Rearview Mirror, a memoir in stories and poems

Cover design by Andrea Gabriel

Be gentle and trust the reflection.
Grief is calling us to open our heart and
nurture what has been shattered by our loss.

You Can Start Anywhere

You can start anywhere.

I'm starting here, my eyes on the last love I watched walk away in the rearview mirror when I dropped him off that night.

Love with hindsight can illuminate a path not seen when facing forward, staring it right in the eyes.

Sometimes love hides.

Love is for keeps, though, even when you try to give it back or run away from it.

It's still yours and it lingers beautifully, even when you don't want it or the person it came with.

Sometimes we hide from love.

I've loved deeply, with commitment and without. Sometimes inconsistently, but maybe that's not exactly true, or even the point.

You can start anywhere.

With your last love or the sound of the sirens outside just now.

You can start by looking at the picture taken when I was about ten, holding my cat Sandy in my arms, hair blowing and the sun shining in my eyes, making me squint.

Looking back through the confusion of childhood, I can see more bright moments than dark. I'm not sure why, but I'm grateful because a series of unfortunate events turned me invisible, immobilized by lies and betrayal, loss, grief, and depression. But like everything in time, the lens shifts and a new story begins. You can start anywhere.

You can start before you knew how cruel people could really be, or before you knew racism was a thing and that its reality would forever touch your life. Before you knew the pain of loss so completely that your body nearly evaporated before your own eyes.

Before it got worse than that.

You can start before you knew self-love and that it would still be there when you had the courage to walk away from what you once thought was love.

Or when the price to be paid was too great for what was offered, and less than what you wanted or deserved.

Knowing that love is both my nature and my choice is a good place to start.

Love doesn't mean you're perfect, that you don't get mad, lose friends, pick unnecessary arguments, or act like an ass sometimes. Love has waltzed me into romance and marriages, raised my children, and guided me on spontaneous trips to animal rescue centers and foreign countries. My adventures with love have been more entertaining, more painful, more impactful, and more surprising than I could have imagined.

Love frames what happens in life and all that we do in a context of our intent to do better, and it keeps us hoping that more good will come our way. And it does.

You can start anywhere.

I'm starting with a look back to see about love and all its wily ways.

New Love

New love and a fresh start.
In midlife, I burned my journals.
Over twenty years into the flames. It made sense.
With my new love, I wanted to travel lightly into the future,
    so certain he was the one I had been waiting for,
    the one who would last the rest of my life,
    despite my history.

I unloaded journals and notebooks from my bookshelves into big, strong black plastic garbage bags and hauled them down the hallway on a bath towel to the fireplace in the living room. Sitting cross-legged on the rug in front of the brick hearth, I took one long, deep breath down into my belly. Let's get this show on the road.

I ceremoniously tore out the pages and tossed them into the flames without reading or cherishing them further. At forty-six, I certainly didn't need detailed reminders of every struggle, kiss, or frustration I had experienced over the previous seven years of living single. I was weary of all that had come before this new love. Putting my heartache in the rearview mirror, I wanted to live in the present. I had studied, workshopped, practiced, and visioned my way here and I liked the reflection I was seeing.

With equal parts haste and hope, I tossed all written record of my day-to-day thoughts into the glowing pulse of the fire. Details about the deaths of two husbands from cancer. My feelings about experiences involving my children and single motherhood. The estrangement from my mother and sister. I burned pictures of past lovers, elements of indecision, considerations I'd grappled with, flashes of Truth with a capital "T," "aha moments," whiny (could be wine-y) rants, and WTF-was-I-thinking doubts that sometimes rode on the coattails of my certainty. Conversations with God. Pages stained with tears of shame, hate, and harm. Breakups with friends and family, men who made the grade, then didn't, men who soured but left a sweet taste, men whom I ignored completely. Relationships—the kind that lasted a minute or a lifetime—either way landing with excruciating detail on the page. Goodbye to the old and welcome to my new, happy ending. Burn, baby, burn!

I met Frank one night through a mutual friend's casual, but intentional, introduction. We enjoyed a fun evening out and I felt a flutter of interest, but he was in a relationship. Respectfully, we didn't exchange numbers. Six months passed and his circumstances changed, at which point he asked our mutual friend if I was open to him calling me. Of course I was.

I thought he was good-looking—handsome, really: well dressed, physically active, big smile, loved to have fun, and knew how to make reservations. On our first date, we took in the spectacular views from the fifty-second floor of San Francisco's Bank of America building. We started with sexy martinis served in small carafes chilling beside short, stemmed glasses on shaved ice beds at window seats in the bar of the Carnelian Room. Dinner followed in the dining room with red wine, breathtaking views, and their incomparable Grand Marnier souffle for dessert. We ended the evening at a concert with the friends who had introduced us. We were off to a great start.

From there, we fell in love quickly. I trusted him and shrugged off my initial reservations about his occupation as a police officer. I was uncomfortable at first—as a woman who stood for peace and a world free of guns and violence—but I could feel into Frank's heart and it was good. The ashes of my journals cooled, and Frank moved in a couple of months later.

While we chose to live together early in our relationship, the timing was a thoughtful decision on my part. I was always intentional about the well-being of my children. I saw that Frank and the men in his family were good and believed our love was sincere and for the long term. I felt that my twelve-year-old son would be in good hands and under a good influence.

I made room in my life and my home for his big, fun-loving family. Of Filipino and African American descent, his family loved good food, cooking, and celebrating together. They demonstrated respect and generational family connection in a way I had longed for most of my life, spending their time together camping, boating, fishing, skiing, biking, cooking, and toasting one another's successes during grace at every gathering. They laughed and joked often, cared deeply for one another, and seemed to accept their respective differences. Frank had been raised in the Pentecostal Church where his mother was the minister, but his family did not hold his secular ways against him. Because of their acceptance, I felt comfortable exploring their beliefs, and one time attended a huge Pentecostal women's weekend event with his mom, sister, sister-in-law, and some other church ladies. Not my way, but where there is love, I'm happy.

Frank had three sons around the ages of my two kids. Our two youngest sons were twelve and thirteen and our three older, mostly launched kids were in their early twenties. Suddenly my house was full of testosterone and male activities: boys roughhousing, washing cars, playing music, and plotting their next pranks, their teasing voices razzing each other and making us laugh.

Marriage seemed our next step. While my friend Gwen and I were out one afternoon, we met Frank at a restaurant for lunch. Prankster that she was, Gwen jokingly mentioned having seen a pair of shoes she thought might be perfect for our wedding. With a smile, Frank said, "Buy the shoes!" A couple of months later, we were designing our wedding rings with a jeweler in Carmel.

It was the fullness of this love that allowed me to release my journals into the fire. By burning the words I'd written in my past, I was burning my past—not so much to eliminate the history of my travails but to make room for new growth. According to Native tradition, intentional fires would be lit across landscapes to encourage the healthy rebirth of tired soil and tangled vegetation, and in many spiritual traditions, fire is recognized as a symbol of awakening. I thought that by reducing the written record of my memories to ash, I could encourage the creation of new, happy memories with Frank. With my struggles, disappointments, grief, and inner transformational work now behind me, it seemed time to write my happy ending.

But first, a little about my journey before the fire.

ACT 1

Love As I Heard It

Bernice was engaged to a man named George, a doctor on military leave returning to service one gray Seattle morning in October 1947. On their way to the train station, Bernice and George stopped at their friend Becky's house for last-minute goodbyes. While the three friends were having coffee, Becky's brother, Hugh, unexpectedly dropped by. Hugh gallantly offered Bernice and George a ride to the train station. On the platform, the couple exchanged what would be their last kiss, because six weeks later, on December 2, 1947, Bernice married Hugh.

Ten months later, I was born.

A small family wedding was held at the home of the bride's parents in Bellingham, Washington. The bride wore a soft blue satin gown and headpiece. In the black-and-white wedding photos, my mother looked beautiful and happy. The blue satin dress hung in the back of my mother's closet for years. It was a safe space where I would hide, dream, and touch something softer than my mother's unaccountably remote attitude. My childhood confusion hung in the folds of that dress and was doomed to hang around in me as I grew up trying to make sense of things no one in my family was willing to discuss.

My mother was a registered nurse with a Bachelor of Science degree from the University of Washington. She was the first in her family of Norwegian immigrants to attend college and was proud of her accomplishments. She worked as the supervisor of labor and delivery at Swedish Hospital, where I was born, and for Dr. Rutherford, the ob-gyn who delivered me. My mother's friends gave her a hard time for getting pregnant so quickly, especially since she was a nurse and had access to the latest information on 1948-style birth control. She called me a "diaphragm baby," which seemed to indicate "unplanned," and over time, I translated it to mean "unwanted."

So it was that two strangers had a baby before knowing each other a full year. I suspect that lust got the better of my parents, hence their hasty marriage. All her life, appearances remained important to my mother. She wanted to make it clear to her kids that she was a virgin when they'd married and that they had been married for more than nine months before my birth. Seventeen years later, when she married her second husband, she practically claimed virginity again, but her children just laughed at her prudishness. I was onto her by then.

When my father was thirteen, his parents divorced, a rarity among that generation. His father had developed a relationship with a new woman and moved on, taking my father's eleven-year-old sister, Becky, with them. My father was left behind with his mother, Helen. Though Helen went on to marry a second and third time and led a vibrant, accomplished life, the loss of her "happy home" and her first marriage in Seattle remained a burden and heartache that followed her until her death at ninety-six.

Aunt Becky was raised by her father and the "other woman," who turned out to be a kind and lovely grandmotherly type. During my childhood, she mailed us delicious homemade raspberry jam and roasted hazelnuts from their Oregon farm at Christmastime. I loved her warmth, her Collie dog, Tam, who ran about the sloping, grassy yard, and the baby chickens she taught us to hold gently when I was four. From this "other woman" I always felt loved and accepted—no strings attached.

My parents moved from Seattle to San Francisco when I was six months old, which situated us closer to my paternal grandmother, Helen, and her second husband, Grandpa Joe. Two years later my sister, Barb, was born. After several reported miscarriages, my mother gave birth to a son, Billy, born three months prematurely.

As I heard it, my parents married for love—for a connection that burned fast and bright. However, as I started piecing together the timeline of their marriage and my arrival into this world, I wondered how much of their union was for love and how much of it was for keeping up appearances—for fear of the consequences of forbidden sex before marriage. By all outward indications, we became a picture-perfect family: two married parents, three kids, two cars, and a house in suburbia. In the maintenance of my mother's exacting image, I wasn't sure how I fit into the frame—beyond my attempts to mind the rules.

Love As I Remember It

Until I was four and a half, we lived in a flat on Seal Rock Drive just blocks from Ocean Beach and across the street from Sutro Park, where a pair of concrete lion statues guarded the entry and captured my heart. I rolled in the sand, picked the bright pink flowers from the ice plant, and received shots at UCSF Hospital to ward off the sand fleas that continually ate away at my tender skin.

Before I started kindergarten, my parents purchased a home on Parrott Drive in San Mateo, California. It was a new development carved through the hills, disrupting the wildlife for years to come. When the door of the dishwasher was opened, terrified mice clung to the racks, staring out, frozen. Snakes slithered through backyards and cars and boys on bikes ran them over in the street. Mountain lions were periodically spotted prowling around. Through grammar school, diamondback rattler heads and tails in mayonnaise jars of formaldehyde were typical show-and-tell treasures. Horses and cows grazed in the fields behind the one long road of houses. At the very end of the road was a field, often muddy, and a sign that announced: SAFEWAY COMING. The store was built about ten years later.

I loved growing up and feeling safe and free whenever I was outside. No house keys. Lots of other children. *Be home before dark* or *stay within "earshot"* in case you got called in sooner. A sandwich, carrots, apples, a jump rope for a bridle, and we could be gone all day. Hop on the back of a horse and ride. We never learned who owned those horses, but we cared for them with a good brushing after every ride, then watched them disappear over the hill until we whistled them back the next day.

Throughout my early life, Grandma Helen would show up— awkward and unannounced—opening the trunk of her Cadillac to reveal unwanted gifts from what we called "the closet." Everything from "the closet" seemed unclean and had a peculiar, musty smell, most of it used and of uncertain origin, much of it left behind by tenants in the Sussex Arms hotel that my grandmother leased and managed for thirty-five years. My father objected to her "bringing us that crap." But every now and then, we'd hit the jackpot, like when we discovered the costumes from members of the Ringling Bros. and Barnum & Bailey Circus who'd supposedly run off in a hurry from the hotel. Best dress-ups ever, with lacy, wired bodices—way bigger than my still-flat chest—made of jewel-colored satin and rows of tulle hugging the high-cut bottoms. I took the lingerie-like costumes from our garage to my girlfriend's playhouse up the street before my dad could get rid of them and we pranced around playing circus, all sexy-like, until we got caught by her mom. And just like that, our too-adult circus finery was flung into the garbage.

Grandma lived in her fancy 1960s-decorated apartment on the ground floor of her "hotel." She liked to show me her beautiful possessions and I loved seeing them in return: sets of elegant china and delicate crystal, smooth monkeypod bowls from her frequent trips to Hawaii, large cut-glass sculptures, jewelry, furs, and peignoir sets. "If you're a good little girl, Krissy, dear," she would say when she caught me admiring her treasures, "it will be yours one day." From early childhood into my teens, the association between my behavior and her promised rewards made it harder for me to compliment her on these displays. I felt manipulated before I even knew the word. She held the strings to her belongings like a puppeteer, and becoming "good enough" seemed ever more impossible to me.

I would be a young adult before my grandmother gave me something without those strings attached. Surprisingly, it was her love and acceptance. Later, it was her 1963 red Cadillac convertible.

Love in the Land of Rules

As my feet dangled under the kitchen table, with my napkin properly placed across my lap, a song slipped through my lips.

"No singing at the dinner table!" my mother scolded.

Where I'm from, love had rules, lots of rules, and those rules were meant to be followed. The rules left no room for self-expression, play, or negotiation. Minding the rules was paramount. When the rules made no sense to me, my parents offered no explanations or allowances for discussion. "Why?" hung in the air, ignored, or was answered with a brusque "Because I said so."

Meanwhile, adults could lie, drink too much, pretend they hadn't, and avoid the perceptions of a curious child. "Mommy, what's wrong?"

"Nothing, everything is fine."

Everything was perpetually fine until it wasn't.

I was a spirited little girl, carefully groomed to meet the 1950s standards of "pleasing and acceptable"—to everyone but me. To my parents, this meant disciplining some of that spirit out of me or hiding it behind good manners and an impeccable appearance. So managed, I did not feel seen most days. More often, I felt confused.

Where I'm from, adults dressed to impress or as close to it as they could afford, and women kept their knees and ankles together, carefully concealed by their skirts. Once they braved a shorter hemline for the sake of fashion, they still covered their knees appropriately with their napkins. Women wearing pants was still a rarity, even while cleaning the house.

We were told to stand when an adult entered the room, to speak politely when spoken to, and to never address an adult by his or her first name without being invited to do so first.

Manners in my family were taught at a young age and included how to hold your fork and knife properly and where to place them to indicate you had completed your meal. How to set the table by orienting placement of each utensil, salad plate, bread-and-butter plate, water glass, and goblet according to its shape and purpose.

We were also taught to stand and sit up straight, to wait until the host or hostess picked up a fork to begin eating, to refrain from talking with food in our mouths, to chew quietly with our mouths closed, to never slurp or lick our fingers, and to keep our elbows out of sight. "Mabel, Mabel, strong and able, keep those elbows off the table!"

As my friend Pat Olsen reminds us in *The Hindsight Handbook*, a little book of wisdom she wrote for her nieces, "Good table manners largely go unnoticed. Bad table manners are impossible to ignore." In other words, I'm not saying these lessons lacked value. They have served me well. And when considering what to teach my children, I taught them manners too—at least those that struck me as relevant or helpful.

What I wanted for my children was that they learn to think for themselves, to remember who they are, and to believe that they were born with gifts to give and talents to express. I wanted them to know that they matter and that their feelings and desires are instructive, and that what inspires them is critical to their well-being and zest for life.

Hard as I worked at being a good girl, my independent nature presented a challenge for my mother, and—despite my cheerful disposition—I managed to get into trouble with some regularity. I woke up in the morning with a smile, hugged my orange cat, Sandy, and carried him down the hall through the kitchen and outside into the backyard. I'd let him go and he'd make a fast getaway over the fence and up the dry, grassy hill. He was free. I was not. I went back inside to dress for school, then onto the tall kitchen stool for my mom to brush my long, blond hair. She pulled it into tight braids, commanding each strand to remain in place until I returned home later in the day.

"Ouch, you're hurting me." *Bop* came the brush, reverberating against my head like a cymbal.

"You have to suffer to be beautiful," my mom said. "Sit still."

It was hard to smile with my hair tugged so tight, but it was class picture day in kindergarten.

I was excited getting off the bus. Before entering the classroom, I knelt to open my lunch box and pull out my hidden treasure. My mother had forbidden me to wear the large green rhinestone brooch from my dress-up box, but I was sure it would liven up my class photo. I'd tucked it in my lunch box before leaving home. I pinned it proudly onto my faded but starched red-and-white-striped dress and ran into the classroom.

I was thrilled the day the pictures were handed out. There I was in the middle of the second row, hands folded neatly in my lap as instructed, my gaudy green accessory on full display. My kindergartener's mind had not yet acquired the skills to ponder future consequences, but I was intent on having things my way. This insistence on venturing in my own direction often meant soap in my mouth, a brush to the side of my head, or a slap on my bare butt. But I continued to venture out regardless.

Photographs of my mother laughing or demonstrating affection toward her children were rare, if they existed at all. In the ones I recall, Barb and I stood on either side of her like bookends clutching our Christmas dolls, Easter baskets, or first-day-of-school lunches. Mom sat with her hands properly folded in her lap. As Billy grew, she propped him up with one arm around his waist, enough to ensure he stayed erect, her other arm dangling at her side.

Coming from the land of rule-based, conditional love, I had to break a few of those rules, pick some fights, and stand my ground. I needed to find my way into an authentic life I could love. Now, when a song slips through my lips, especially at dinner, I sing it with a nod to Mom and a big smile. *It's much more delicious this way!*

Mommy Love

We liked to ask for things we couldn't have.

Popsicles, candy bars, Oreos, and Bosco.

Sometimes my sister and I were allowed to sit on the magazine rack near the store entry and read comic books while our mother shopped.

Maybe if we were good little girls, one of those treats might make a surprise landing in the cart as she efficiently wheeled up and down the aisles of Shop-Rite market.

She was frugal yet gourmet, and even her warmed-up leftovers tasted and looked better than most other moms' fresh-from-the-can '50s-style cooking.

She could bake too. Her rhubarb and lemon meringue pies were my favorites, and her angel food cake, always my birthday request.

Vases held artfully arranged weeds and wildflowers from the hillside.

The chairs were secondhand: an overstuffed red one with a gold, scratchy thread, a faded green wool wingback, and a yellow patio lounger.

A twin bed with a slipcover and bolster for a couch, and a round, painted pine coffee table, once the Norwegian family dining table until my dad sawed the legs off.

Family lore reported that they couldn't afford chairs as a young
married couple, so they sat on floor cushions. Young, re-
sourceful, and spry.

Big picture windows looked out into the backyard, always a
work in progress, with glorious tulips and daffodils as place-
holders for landscaping yet to come.

She knew the name of every tree and flower.

Dust was gathered while still floating in the sunbeams, and yet I
crawled on hands and knees with a dust cloth through the
chair rungs and carved dining room table legs every Saturday
morning.

No rings in her tub.

No odors in her toilets.

No hair out of place on my head.

Soap in my mouth until I tasted blood for talking back.

How can an artist come alive while held captive in such fine order?

Easy. Do as you're told, become their version of you, and rebel
later.

Daddy Love

My daddy was the fun parent, and I was his "pal." As a young girl,
I'd wash the cars on the weekend with him, working those scuffed
white wall tires spotless with an SOS pad while he jested about
my mother's parallel parking skills. "Let's go, sport!" he'd say, and
off we'd go for a fast ride to dry the car off. Our trip usually included a stop downtown at the Rose Room, where he swigged a
drink or two at the bar and I got to pick cheese and olives and
cherry peppers from the smorgasbord to accompany my Shirley

Temple. We'd drive home up windy Parrott Drive having had a wonderful adventure.

On Sunday mornings, I would settle onto Daddy's lap, and he would clip my fingernails and read me the funnies in the *San Francisco Chronicle*. His favorites were *Dennis the Menace*, *Blondie*, and *Beetle Bailey*, but he read them all and I wouldn't let him skip a single one. My sixth birthday dinner at the Circus Room in the Fairmont Hotel introduced me to live music, where we saw the inimitable Marilyn Maxwell perform. While she was up on stage, her shoe strap broke. She kicked off the other shoe and kept right on singing and dancing. Why they took me there to see her, I'll never know, but I delighted in the experience.

Daddy gave me my first three records: the soundtrack from *Oklahoma!* and two forty-fives: Sheb Wooley's "The Purple People Eater" and Sam Cooke's "You Send Me." The stereo lived in my parents' bedroom, hardly making music central to our home, but one day Daddy brought home a large, fancy radio that sat out of reach on top of the mantel in the living room. Mostly it played KABL, a canned elevator Muzak station of days gone by. Rarely classical or rock 'n' roll. It didn't seem to add to the household fun or enjoyment. Rather, it was just one more example of weirdly expensive items that appeared in our house without explanation.

Often on Sundays, Grandma Helen and Grandpa Joe would drive from San Francisco for dinner. It wouldn't be long before the arguments started, usually just as she arrived and opened the trunk of her Cadillac, directing Grandpa to bring in some of the tenants' random items from the Sussex Arms hotel.

On those Sunday visits, Daddy would usually go out to the backyard and pull up a stool by the barbecue, where he simmered and watched the coals burn down. I would go with him and sit quietly. I loved my daddy and always sided with him. Having no idea what the problem really was, but sensitive to his anger, I avoided staying inside with my complicated mother and offending grandmother, both smoldering while acting like everything was just fine. With Daddy, I knew where I stood.

When it was time for dinner, we'd sit at the dining room table, perfectly set with the silverware lined evenly one inch from the table's edge. My dad would then turn the black-and-white console television around to make it visible from the dining table. This happened only on Sundays when Grandma Helen was there. Otherwise, we were never allowed to watch television during meals. Grandma would have to see panelists guess what each guest did for a living on the old game show *What's My Line?* before driving back to the city to turn on the heat at the hotel. The blare of the television also served to eliminate any further conversation.

When I was about ten, my dad took my sister and me on individual trips to Disneyland. He had an office in Los Angeles, and once or twice the family would take a summer vacation to Newport Beach for a week or two while he worked. But this time I went by myself for a few days. We had a great time on the rides. Nobody could spin the teacups on the Mad Tea Party faster than my daddy, but that night he went out, leaving me alone in the motel. I was scared, but I don't remember asking him not to go or having a choice in the matter. I pretended to be asleep when he came back later to check on me and had a woman with him. In a little treasure box from my childhood, I still have the Tinker Bell necklace he bought me on that trip.

One day in eighth grade, a boy I knew menacingly told me that my dad had been drunk and crashed into a tree in their front yard the night before. I rushed to Daddy's defense.

"Yeah, he was walking around, didn't even know his name," the boy said.

"That's not true! My dad is out of town on a business trip. You're a liar!"

That evening, my mother took us to the hospital after school to see my father. He had the imprint of the steering wheel on his chest and a bandage on his head where he had hit the metal frame of his convertible T-Bird. I cried as he cautioned me, "You should never believe everything you read in the paper or what other people tell you, sport."

"But, Daddy, he said you didn't know your name and you were drunk."

"I had just bumped my head. I wasn't drunk."

So who was lying this time? It hurt to know it was my dad when I overheard him admit to having stopped at the Rose Room on his way home. Women in his life, alcohol, and knowing my dad was lying contributed to my uncertainty about whom to trust and how to manage in the adult world I was growing up in. It didn't help that this kind of male behavior was normalized in 1961. "Boys will be boys."

Sister Love

The sweetest thing I remember about my sister is her telling me bedtime stories. She was an avid reader. Since we went to our twin beds each night at about the same time—in a room we shared for fifteen years—I would ask her what she was reading, and she would stop to tell me all about it. It was like getting bedtime stories when I was big, and long after our parents had quit reading to us. It felt so generous. We both became avid readers.

As children, we occasionally pushed our beds together and made forts out of our blankets, trying to whisper while giggling before our father shouted, "Be quiet and go to sleep!" Next, we heard his thundering footsteps coming down the hall to break up the fun.

Over the years, we stopped playing together and somehow lost our heart connection. I'm not sure how or why or when our discord even started. Maybe we were born that way. At times, I thought my rebellious insistence with my parents might clear a pathway, somehow making things easier for her or saving her the trouble of fighting for what she wanted. But our ways were different, and she didn't need me to make her way easier. Perfection was her superpower. My rebellion was of no use to her.

By high school, our differences were hard to ignore. She had surpassed me by becoming the model daughter. Perfect makeup and outfit choices, good grades, nothing out of line—and a mystery to me. As my girlfriends and I sang rock 'n' roll, we'd tease and mock her operatic-sounding voice and occasional slip into the British accent she had developed out of the blue. Then we attended her college opera performance recital and were humbled by the beauty of her accomplishment.

Unfortunately, Barb and I shared only occasional and situational appreciation for each other. She remained more fun than anyone when it came to going off a diet, gleefully whipping up a chocolate cake with frosting and preparing a feast. She stayed with me a couple of summers while she was in grad school, moving in with me to work in San Francisco and save money. We tried to get to know each other, and at times we appeared close. She possessed a biting, clever sarcasm—entertaining but intermittently mean-spirited. While it was true that I judged her seeming perfection, her painful disdain frequently pushed me away. Perhaps jealousy played into our distance. Perhaps she observed my parents' criticism of me and believed it to be true. Or maybe we just never really liked each other. Whatever the reasons, she steered clear of a relationship with me, preferring to judge me from a distance.

Separate Ways

Could the portraits tell the story even then?
The summer of 1958 spent sitting.
The artist, a friend of my father's,
but a stranger to us, who supposedly painted us to repay a debt.
And so we sat while summer happened without us that year.

We sat in matching dresses that turned blue on the canvas.
I preferred the sophistication of the true colors of the dress,
champagne taffeta and black velvet.
Serious young faces took shape.
She hated her hair.
I wondered how he could see me and
what the future would hold for that girl.

The portraits hung, side-by-side.
Sisters in separate frames
creating separate ways even then.
Sisters who tried a few times, but never became friends.
Sisters whose only bond was biology.
Sisters framed young.
Eager to fly free of the other.

Sisters with disconnected hearts and minds.
Hearts that never mended.
Portraits that hang in storage, dusted with past bitterness.
Blue dresses and champagne sipped worlds apart.
And when I called, I didn't like the one who answered.

Angel Love

Our youngest brother, Billy, was born when I was nine years and four months old. I'm specific, because that's the age when I first realized how serious life was, and how fragile. He was three months premature and weighed three pounds, seven ounces, but later dropped to less than two pounds. He was diagnosed with cerebral palsy and was visually impaired because of the over-oxygenation of incubators in 1958. He remained in the hospital for the first three months until he weighed five pounds and came home then only because my mom was a registered nurse. Billy was called a "miracle baby." In the face of fear, I believe love is the miracle: it can heal circumstances, broken hearts—even bodies.

Billy's tiny body, however, could not yet breathe and swallow at the same time. He lay lengthwise on his back in my mother's lap, his head at her knees. She held a small bottle to his mouth, and he drank for as long as he was able. Sitting on the floor at my mother's side, I watched for the moment when he began to turn blue, indicating that he had stopped breathing. Setting the bottle aside, my mother would rub his little feet, tap lightly on his chest, and raise him up on her shoulder to get him breathing again. The goal for this lengthy process was to complete a small feeding and keep Billy alive at the same time.

Once she had finished feeding Billy, my mother would lay him in his bassinette in the extra bedroom we had just begun to convert into a nursery. I would pull up my rocking chair and stay by his side. I wanted to watch him breathe. Sitting with him in the quiet, I became aware of the angels surrounding him. These angels brought me so much comfort in ways I could not share with my parents or sister. I felt alone with my fear, but sitting near the bassinette, I knew that Billy and I shared the angels' love.

It wasn't long before I became part of Billy's care team. I was serious and unstoppable. I learned to feed Billy, change his diapers, and eventually, help with his daily care and frequent post-surgical needs. At eighteen months old, he was one of the youngest people to begin wearing contact lenses. For years, Mom or I would take turns gently parting his tight little eyelids and placing the hard bits of plastic over his irises, then repeating the process in reverse before he went to sleep, ensuring the hard lenses were put into a special solution and "cooked" overnight to clean. Billy had numerous surgeries on his eyes and legs throughout his childhood. He wore braces of many varieties, sizes, and shapes—all specified and designed toward helping him learn how to walk, which he did at almost five years old. He struggled mightily with balance but managed to walk on his own until he hit his thirties and began relying full-time on a wheelchair.

Billy attended Easterseals nursery school and then received academic instruction, as well as physical and occupational therapy at El Portal Elementary School. I volunteered at his school, helping out wherever I was needed. I loved working with the children and being surrounded by compassionate school staff—people who gave me a glimpse into the importance of meaningful work. When I was old enough, I volunteered as a candy striper in both a nursing home and the hospital where Billy had been born. Once

I got my first real job in a clinical laboratory, I continued to explore medical career choices throughout my life—always seeking rewarding administrative positions and professional and personal growth I could not have foreseen at this young age.

While I was volunteering at Billy's school, I briefly considered occupational therapy as a career choice, having previously rejected the idea of becoming a nurse. I'd made this decision while moving books from the shelves in Billy's nursery and flipping open one of my mother's nursing books. Coming across a picture of a child with smallpox, I was inconsolable. I was highly sensitive to others' distress, and the sight of this ravaged child so traumatized me that I ended my nursing career dreams then and there. Of course, even though I never became a nurse, I eventually grew a thicker skin and became interested rather than traumatized by medical conditions and treatments—all of which would serve to benefit my many years on the management side of medicine and my fate as a caregiver at home to loved ones.

Love Dies

On March 25, 1963, during my high school freshman year, I came home to find my mother ironing. She hated to iron and an overflowing basket of clothes typically lay in wait for her. When she could procrastinate no longer, she would set up the ironing board in the living room and distract herself by turning on the black-and-white television or looking out the window while sprinkling and rolling up the cotton clothes, one by one. As the iron heated, she would place each of the prepared laundry items in the refrigerator, taking out a few at a time to stack on the ironing board for pressing. She was attacking stubborn wrinkles in a shirt when I came in that day, plopping into the big red chair nearby. The phone rang and I leaped toward the kitchen to answer, hoping the call was for me.

A mysterious man's voice asked to speak to my mother. "Mom, it's for you." As she came to the phone, something in me slowed as she took the receiver of the yellow wall phone in her hand and raised it to her ear. I hung close by. "Yes, this is she. Yes. Yes." Silence. Then I heard her scream. My mother was not a demonstrative woman and I had only heard her cry twice: late at night while arguing with my dad on the phone, and again the night she went to the hospital to deliver my brother while only six months pregnant and fearing another miscarriage. When she learned that Daddy had died in a plane crash, I saw her cry for the third time.

I don't know who my mother called next or how this horrifying news got around, but suddenly the house filled with neighbors, friends, and people I didn't even know. We were fed an endless stream of casseroles, Jell-O salads, and desserts. I moved through the house, numb. And people kept showing up. My father's younger sister, Aunt Becky, was among them. She and my dad had never been close, but I liked her right away. She was funny, she actually talked to me, and she let me in on her secret: hiding in the bathroom to blow cigarette smoke out the window so her Oregon mother wouldn't know she was smoking. I loved her honesty. It made me feel included as her confidant and co-conspirator. But other visitors felt like intruders. Dr. Peters, the minister from the Presbyterian church we'd casually attended— whom everyone called "doctor," perhaps because he had his doctorate in theology—appeared at our door one day when I went to answer it. I couldn't understand why he was there. He belonged at church, not at our house. Everything was so confusing.

I guess I was in shock. I don't remember where my sister or brother were during that time and I barely recall my mother. I don't remember hugs or grieving together as a family. I went alone to the room that I shared with my sister and turned on the pink radio I'd received as a gift from my dad. For the next few days, I listened to KYA's hourly news, hoping to hear that my father had been found, wandering dazed but alive in the Mojave Desert where the plane had gone down. Then the news was confirmed. My father and his business partner—who had been piloting the plane from Phoenix to Bakersfield—collided midair with a California condor that possessed a thirteen-foot wingspan. All three died instantly, including the condor.

My father had always been strict with me and as I began to mature, he'd been cracking down on me even more. Shortly before he died, I was on my way out to catch the school bus wearing a bright-green-striped shift I had sewn the night before. Knowing he would deem my dress too short, I covered myself in a coat, hoping to sneak out of the house unchallenged. Sure enough, we met in the hall. "What the hell are you wearing?" he said. "I can't see it!" I ran back to my room and tugged a white pleated skirt from my closet, putting it on over my dress. I still ended up grounded for two weeks. He wasn't having it, and had he lived, I'm sure our relationship wouldn't have gotten any easier for him or for me.

I was so afraid that God had killed my father because of his flaws, or worse, because of mine. His love had been the best I'd had. At least it was love I could feel and I trusted, in spite of his imperfections.

I heard these words recently on a Sober Curious podcast: "When I lie to keep the peace, I start a war within myself." It's an inter-generational thing, learning to lie. Lying gets handed down from parents too afraid to speak their personal truths to their kids or to each other. Then the child, having been taught by his or her personal masters of illusion, begins to lie, in turn, to the parents. Ultimately, those same unavailable parents turn their blind eyes to the errant child they've been hiding from all along.

Until I was strong enough to abandon my parents' well-ordered illusions about their lives, I attempted to fit in. But time after time, my internal combustion blew up my facade. Desperate to find the truth behind the words "everything is fine," and the feelings that told me something different, I danced in the mine-fields of their lies and omissions. Then remorse and shame would rein me back in, reminding me of how I was expected to behave and what a disappointment I was.

The family began attending a Presbyterian church when I was about eight or nine—maybe younger, maybe older. I think our churchgoing came not so much from my parents' affinity for re-ligious dogma but a sense of duty to provide their children with at least a Sunday-school level of Protestant education. My dad's latest toy, a transistor radio about the size of a cigarette pack, was often tucked in his shirt pocket, the earphone cord snaking up his neck, quietly playing the baseball game throughout the service.

I volunteered in the church nursery and washed baby toys there once a month on Saturdays, I sang in the youth choir, attended ski trips, and made friends—some that have lasted a lifetime. I was taught to say my prayers before going to sleep. These rote prayers always ended with "God bless Mommy and Daddy, Barb, and Billy." Beyond memorizing "Now I lay me down to sleep, I pray the Lord my soul to keep . . ." which scared the shit out of me—I improvised. My prayers went something like "Please, God, please! Make me fall asleep fast so I can get up from this nap and get back outside to play" or "Make Billy all better" or, later, "Don't let Daddy be dead." I sincerely wished for a visible sign from God that He could handle His part and that everything really would be fine, like my mother always said it was.

At best I was begging for the elusive change I wished for. At worst I was bartering with Santa Claus. Either way, I became enveloped in guilt, shame, and hopelessness. That punitive old God in the sky, his bony finger pointed at me, seemed hard to argue with, along with His message that I just wouldn't be able to measure up. Things were not going to go my way. The war within me began with my parents, then comingled with God, misunderstood dogma, and my family's insincere religiosity and absence of spiritual candor. My father's death and the way it was explained to me only added to my existential confusion and uncertainty.

Love's Lineage

I am from a quiet, cold lineage of women.
I am from laughter through tight, pursed lips.
I am from a terse smile and closed arms.

I am from forever hold your tongue and tone it down.

I am from go to bed, be quiet, and take your cat with you.

I am from stop crying or I'll give you something to cry about.

I am from borrowed dresses and put a smile on that face.

I am from last call, last dance, last dad home.

I am from you can't have that, but you'd better keep trying.

I am from you'll never live up to your potential and you have to suffer to be beautiful.

I am from the deepest well of sorrow and uncertainty and lights out.

I am also from beauty. Daffodils, tulips, and hillside thistles, fast cars, roller skates, and sparkling stars,

I am from acacia trees and eucalyptus, red tailed hawks, and shiny, feathered crows,

I am from bright blue skies with puffy clouds the shape of bunnies and dragons.

I am attracted to the more colorful, lively way.

My parents communicated the need for me to "tone it down" in a million little ways, confirmed by their efforts to enroll me in an all-girls Catholic high school in their hope the nuns would discipline me into submission and cultivate a less buoyant personality.

I was sensitive, rebellious, curious, and lining up as one of my generation who would "question authority" and wear the button proudly. But I wasn't a "bad girl," which seemed to be their fear, or a "slut," as a seventh-grade physical education teacher called me when I ran after a baseball sailing onto the girls' field and threw it back to the boys. I was sent to the principal and my parents were called in for my insubordinate behavior. My parents must have been genuinely concerned, but I knew my innocence and was angry and confused by their lack of trust in me. Was it so important for me to stay in line—the one society drew and defined—a line my parents seemed compelled to enforce? Would they sooner turn me over to some religion they didn't believe in, practice, or align with in principle? That Catholic God and his nuns must have been some kind of powerful to their minds.

I passed the Catholic school's entrance exam and attended the orientation, but a lot of smart Catholic girls passed the exams and made the cut ahead of me that year, so this young heathen heaved a sigh of relief when she got placed on a waiting list. I would never cross the threshold of Notre Dame High School again.

That kind of parental fear for who you are and who you will grow up to become must be terrifying. Living under that umbrella of fear breeds deep, inexplicable, and unspeakable shame, toxic niceness, and a stifling need for perfection.

Love's First Funeral and What Came Next

My father's funeral was closed-casket. It would be the first for me in a long line of funerals. The church overflowed with flowers unlike any I had ever seen: huge red and white rose hearts with outstretched banners my grandmother had provided that read "LOVING SON" and "LOVING HUSBAND." Maybe one banner read "LOVING FATHER," but I don't remember that one. Ostentatious baskets of gladiolas filled the dais and would remain my least favorite flower. An American flag was draped over the casket in honor of Daddy's service in the US Navy, and he was buried in the Golden Gate National Cemetery along with other veterans. At the gravesite, gunshots rang out. Uniformed young men folded the flag and handed it to my mother. The attendees retreated in their black suits and veils. Those who attended Daddy's funeral included his girlfriend at the time—a woman whose name I don't recall. I would learn about Daddy's girlfriend later from Junie, a family friend, auntie of my heart, and my biggest champion and most "for-real person" I would know from childhood until she died. I wore the turquoise silk-sheath dress with a tiny print, long sleeves, and a tie belt that I had worn for Christmas three months earlier when I'd felt dressed up and chic. At the funeral, I felt uncomfortable and squirmy. Even the dress made me sad.

That night, our family went out to dinner. The evening was confusing with all the disparate grandparents, previously unknown relatives, and this new and entertaining aunt and the five cousins she'd told me about. The cousins sounded perfect: good-looking, smart, liked by their parents and our grandparents, and disappointing to no one. I began to sense that my side of the family didn't quite measure up. I obstinately ordered sauteed frog legs and was chastised for pushing my food around the plate.

My father's watch was never found in the wreckage of the plane, so the house insurance paid my mother for the loss. The life insurance company claimed that his policy did not cover "Acts of God" and paid nothing. I spiraled and became an atheist. *What kind of God would kill my father?* I heard the explanations: "God must have needed him" and "God had big plans for him" and "God's plans cannot be questioned." None of these pronouncements made sense. Condolences and rationalizations from well-meaning people were of no comfort. If anything, they only added to my confusion about God and my daddy. In subsequent years, my head would snap around at shadows of men with crew cuts or curly red hair, even men who looked nothing like Daddy but drove by in a white 1963 Thunderbird like his.

Before the reordering of family life, and before I felt recovered in any meaningful way, the world joined me in stunned horror over the sudden, violent death of then-President Kennedy on November 22, 1963. Just eight months after my father's death at forty-two, while I was changing in the locker room for phys-ed class, the announcement came over the school's PA system. "At forty-six years old, John Fitzgerald Kennedy, the thirty-fifth president of the United States, has been assassinated while riding in a motorcade in Dallas, Texas." The loss of the illusion of stability and safety was devastating and long-lived. I was in awe of former first lady Jacqueline Kennedy's composure, grace, and dignity, and I couldn't help but notice how lovingly she related to her children. I pondered the source of her strength, and then—like most people—I returned to my life with all its sorrow, grief, and uncertainty corralled within.

Because my father's parents were divorced, two sets of paternal grandparents battled over who would be most effective in helping my mother sort out Daddy's business affairs. My grandmother Helen claimed—with bankbook notations to support her revelations—that she had been making payments on our house without my mother's knowledge and that my father was in far more financial trouble than my mother had realized. Offers were made to resolve the debt.

In the end, probably owing to fifteen years of dealing with my grandmother's manipulation and my father's deceit, my mother chose my dad's father as her adviser. Less than a year after my dad died, we moved to a small, rented house, leaving behind the home I loved and the dining room furniture and master bedroom set— "gifts" from my grandmother, I would learn. Another gift that didn't make the move was a Christmas present my grandmother had given my mother the year before. Beautifully gift-wrapped, the present held the promise of something my mother might love but could never afford for herself. We were excited about what might be in that box. It turned out to be an impersonal and wildly disappointing watermelon platter and became the source of a family joke—one we laughed about behind my grandmother's back, of course. Then one day, while helping us pack for the move, Auntie June looked at my mom devilishly and smashed the hated platter on the dining room floor. This joyous moment of destruction provided a little levity during an otherwise painful task.

With the move, I had to change high schools after Christmas break in my sophomore year. I was angry and hated to leave my friends; no one had anything complimentary to say about my grandmother, and I'd begun to absorb their negativity. The lesson for me was that "money trumped love" and that my feelings didn't matter. Later that year, I told Grandma Helen never to call me again. I would not be bribed by her or her money. She persisted by continuing to reach out and occasionally showing up without notice or invitation. Some years later, I capitulated and we began to explore an honest relationship.

To my disgust—and in his new role as my mother's adviser—my paternal grandfather began making regular visits from Oregon. He was a bigoted braggadocio and a blowhard I didn't like or trust. I recoiled from his negative remarks and his habit of referring to people by the lowest slang assigned to their race, ethnicity, country, or culture. He would feign reading the paper on the living room couch when he was visiting, deliberately stretching out his legs, and requiring me to ask him to move his feet as I vacuumed on Saturday mornings, eager to get my chores done. I later learned firsthand how he spoke to his church members where he was a deacon and elder, telling the congregation about the "burden" of my mother, as well as my sister, my "crippled" brother, and me—the orphans of his ne'er-do-well son.

A few years later, my grandfather would introduce my mother to a new widower, Ned, formerly a member of his church community and now living in the Bay Area. Ned's wife had died less than a week earlier, but my grandparents were encouraging my mother to put on her lipstick and dress up when he came over. Ned had two sons, ages nineteen and twenty-one, and one twelve-year-old daughter. By this time, I was sixteen, Barb was fourteen, and Billy was seven. The introduction turned out to be a success and Grandpa was happy to dump us. My mother and Grandpa's "friend" Ned were married five months later in April 1966, the day after my senior prom. The newlyweds sat their six children down on the couch and vowed that nothing we ever did would break them up. As a couple, they were invincible, and they came first, no matter what. You see, my mother had friends who had broken up and everyone had blamed the woman's kids. Our parents were not going to let that happen. They made us into believers as we each tried to find our place in the newly merged family.

Two months after the wedding, the day after I graduated from high school, we moved from our house in San Mateo to Ned's house in San Jose. With nothing but *The Brady Bunch*—a corny fantasy show about blended families—as our road map, we all lived in the same house over that summer and did our best to get to know and abide one another.

Bedrooms were reassigned to accommodate all of us. Robert and Jim got the short end and found their twin beds in the laundry room, indicating the space outside the front door was next. Barb and I lucked out and shared the boys' former bedroom with a courtyard entrance I could sneak into quietly providing my sister didn't sound the alarm. Ned's daughter Cappy kept her room, and

Billy, the youngest, got his own room and was "mainstreamed" that fall into public school for the first time.

My thirteen-year-old stepsister, Cappy, quickly found herself caught in the web of Bernice's school of rules: manners and lady-like behavior were established as the new order in the household. My mom cooked continually for eight, introducing my new siblings to a variety of fresh vegetables. She scored a hit with every meal. Those of us old enough to drive vied for Ned's 1965 red Mustang. After Jim got off work and on days when I couldn't get back to the Peninsula to see my friends, we raced through the hills of San Jose in Jim's new 1966 red MG. We all had a lot of fun getting to know one another that strange summer.

For my mother and stepfather, it was Frank Sinatra, gourmet dinners, scotch, and cigarettes—and a fresh start except for the six kids they came with. We were young pieces on their chessboard of life, and it seemed that they wanted to tip the board and start over. But here we were: the leftover pieces from pasts they no longer wanted.

My mother seemed clear about what was required of a wife—like it or not—and was willing to pay the price twice. Consider my mother's late afternoon change of clothes and the application of lipstick in preparation for my father's return from work. His magical arrival could happen at a "reasonable hour," but just as likely occur long after my bedtime. Still, she faithfully prepared and hid any disappointment from me, my sister and brother, and probably everyone else. Once she was married to Ned, my father fell from the unstable pedestal she had placed him on, but she continued to perform her domestic rituals faithfully. I admired her at the time and took note that Ned came home right after work every day. I factored in Ned's timely arrivals as a possible wifely sign of success.

My mother and I had been on a rocky road during my teen years and after my dad died. I often longed to connect with her. When I occasionally felt a hint of her heart opening to me, I gratefully launched myself into that rare, soft space. In a vulnerable moment, I once told her I'd been experiencing some teen angst and then heard her recount my confession laughingly to a friend, trivializing what I had shared. I felt my trust violated, and not for the first time. This instance demonstrated one of the many careless, hurtful ways she made me feel undeserving of her consideration—beyond her rigidly defined duty as my mother.

I would go on to study organizational development and psychology and be introduced to the concept of family systems that revealed behaviors from my mother I couldn't access as a child but always longed to understand. It made me wonder about her deeper wounding and what pain or loss she held or hid from. Why did I always miss her? I missed her when I was too young to realize her emotional absence even while her body was present. Few could say they knew my mother's feelings, and after marrying for the second time, it wouldn't be long before her every opinion came out of Ned's mouth first. What was on her mind and where was her love for her children? Where did she live inside herself, that empty shell she filled with scotch and cigarettes for the last half of her life? She would remain a mystery to me, as would her claim of sharing the "perfect marriage" with Ned.

For the Love of Finding a New Life

I could have been an A student, but I wasn't. By the sixth grade, I walked a delicate tightrope at school, terrified of failure and of disappointing my parents. By the time I reached high school, I was bored. I wrote notes to my friends about my classroom misery, cute boys, or mean girls, and too often got caught passing those notes to others. Red-faced and sullen while the teacher read aloud the confiscated notes, I collapsed in silent embarrassment until the bell rang. Swimming, English, and biology were my favorite subjects. I swam on two swim teams, did all the reading and participated in class, aced most tests, delved into the discussions, the science, and symbology, and never wrote a paper. That strategy kept me at a grade level ranging from a B-minus to a C, with one exception—I flunked golf in my freshman year, incomprehensible to my father (who was still alive then) and my only academic F ever.

My desire to do well in school contradicted my belief that I wasn't smart enough. I had many good friends at several high schools and felt included in those fun, adventurous, and caring circles, but I wanted a different, more independent, grown-up life. I was just ballsy enough to think I was prepared for such a life. Still, I struggled and slipped in and out of believing my parents' worst fears about me. I would never "live up to my potential." I didn't exactly know what that meant or why they thought so poorly of me, but it was a potent prognostication of something lacking and unrecoverable in me. My mother often reminded me about these supposed inadequacies. I understood that some things were just not possible for me, but what I wanted most was to be loved. Getting married and having a baby seemed like my best chance.

I had been babysitting to make money for school clothes and spending my own money since I was eleven. Then I got my first real job as a lab assistant at a medical clinic after school in my junior year. During my senior year of high school, I attended school half days and was at work by one thirty in the afternoon. I hadn't entirely given up the idea of college and went ahead and took the SATs just in case.

A female freshman on campus who worked in the lab with me taught me firsthand about college life and the protest activities as they took off and exploded between 1964 and 1966 at UC Berkeley. I also knew a few kids attending San Francisco State University who experienced similar events during the same two-year stretch. By 1966, the year I graduated from high school, the Black Panther Party was organized in Oakland. I developed peripheral curiosity about the free speech movement, civil rights, and the Vietnam War because boys I knew were getting drafted. But my family of Republicans provided no activists, rebels, or people of color to expand my understanding or support a new curiosity or perspective. I had a lot to learn. Junior college would be the best I could do as a mediocre student who wasn't living up to her potential. *Yep. So much for college: I think I'll get married.*

I was part of the generation of young women who grew up wearing proper wool coats and white gloves to go downtown in San Francisco—in my case, while accompanying my Grandma Helen—a far cry from my jeans and fringed leather jacket soon to come. I longed for the freedom of San Francisco and the restlessness of Berkeley. Fascinated and a little apprehensive, my girlfriends and I drove to Haight-Ashbury, longing to experience Haight Street. It was wild: bumper-to-bumper traffic had everyone cruising at a crawl. Music played and stoned, long-haired strangers pressed their faces against our car windows, smoke billowing a new and unfamiliar smell. The Haight's great social experiment in the '60s lured me beyond my strict, conservative upbringing. When rebellion broke out, the Summer of Love both intrigued and frightened me as the music and chaos filled my body and soul. Rather than run to it and dance, I froze. I also passed on the drugs of the day, which probably secured my ability to stay where I was for as long as I did. The road not taken—a different story lived.

ACT II

It Looks Like Love

Newlywed parents Bernice and Ned went on their honeymoon, and while they were away, I got engaged to my badass boyfriend, Dan. My new brother, Robert, also got engaged. His girlfriend was pregnant. Upon the parents' return, Ned advised Robert to join the navy and get out of town fast. He did and went to Vietnam. New brother Jim got an apartment in San Jose and the youngest three of our newly blended family remained with the parents.

When I think of my first husband, I don't remember loving him, really. More than anything, I remember the desire to love and be loved. But I sure thought it was love while my mother was on her honeymoon during spring break of my senior year, and Dan and I walked into Kay Jewelers and picked out a sweet, tiny diamond wedding set. I don't remember a proposal or any fanfare, but when I returned to school, I dangled my left hand like a giant engagement ring was weighing it down. The prized ring also prompted me to quit biting my fingernails, a nasty, anxious habit I had developed over the years.

I wanted to be a wife and a mother, and as I understood it, these roles had better take place in that order. I had a naive fantasy about what domestic life might be like. *Me with my lipstick on, slim and sexy when my wonderful husband came home from work right on time to the delicious dinner I had lovingly prepared and served on a table just for him. A life of glamour for me—as seen on TV.* Mostly, I wanted to feel deserving of love, as though I never had been before. I turned away from the unknown of college life and reached out for what looked like love and got it.

I met Dan when I was sixteen during the summer before my senior year in high school. My girlfriends Candy and Sharon had just graduated and gotten their own apartment. With no curfew, I was out having fun and spending the night with them as often as I could get away. We met Dan and a bunch of his friends while we were all cruising down El Camino, the guys showing off their hot rods. They signaled us to pull over and talk and we did. Over the next few weeks, we met up and paired up in the way romance happened back then. I actually liked one of the other guys better, but Dan was the one paying attention to me. He was nineteen, a rough-and-tumble high school dropout and a fast-driving, knowledgeable auto mechanic with a preference for Chevys. He taught me to drive his hot rod, had serious anger management issues before I knew the term or what I was in for, lied a lot as I would come to realize, and he had no job. Surprise—my mother didn't like him. *Fine with me!*

Hoping, maybe even believing, marriage would be my golden ticket, I married Dan on the one-year anniversary of our first real date, just two weeks after my eighteenth birthday. I thought he supplied the most immediate path to the adult life I was envisioning: a dog, three children (two boys and a girl), and a house in a nice neighborhood. We would rent out the first house when we upgraded and purchased the second. I figured all of this would take about six years, maybe seven. I had nothing in mind beyond that.

Before those children manifested, I became afraid. I had seen Dan threaten, demean, fight, and—more than once—jump out of his car to attack a driver who mistakenly crossed his path, scaring me and everyone around. I didn't condone or excuse his awful behavior, but unthinkable as it is for me now, I managed to overlook a lot of it while living in the land of no self-esteem or self-worth. I set aside my fears, reasoning that I had gone far enough in the direction of my dream toward love and being loved, and Dan had made himself available to me when it seemed as though no one else ever would. Naive and stupid as it sounds, and despite all indications to the contrary, I couldn't imagine Dan turning his madness and machismo toward me.

My mother and new stepfather of six months paid for our modest wedding at Carmel's Highlands Inn. I wore a beautiful, embossed white satin cocktail-length dress with a matching Nehru collared coat. Very Jackie Kennedy! My mother and I shopped together for the ensemble, which included white satin slingback heels and a small, short veil hanging from a circle of faux flowers: fake but pretty.

The night before my wedding I picked up my maid of honor, Candy, and we arrived home twenty minutes after my curfew—midnight on Saturdays. I was stunned to find my mother up waiting for me and furious. The absurdity! I softened when I realized why she was so angry. She had planned on having a "birds and bees" conversation on the eve of my wedding. It hadn't occurred to me that she had anything more to impart since her first and last words to me regarding sex had been at around age eleven and were along the lines of "sex is something nice for married people."

We didn't get much further that night. "I wanted to see if you had any questions," she said.

"No, Mom. But thanks."

In attendance at the wedding were my mother, stepfather, siblings, and maid of honor, and Dan's parents, sister, and best man,

Ralph. Auntie Tina, my favorite aunt and my mother's oldest sister, must have insisted on coming, because my mother was adamant about not counting this wedding as an event we were celebrating. Fifteen guests were there in total, including the bride and groom. We toasted Martinelli's apple cider with a cake and might have served appetizers. My parents were surely visiting the bar for scotch but wouldn't have extended their generosity by offering my new in-laws a drink. They were barely polite to Dan's parents, as I recall. The only wedding photo I remember is a candid shot of me with a cigarette in my hand standing alone by the hotel's wishing well.

We didn't have the luxury of a honeymoon night at the Highlands Inn. (It would be years before I would stay at the Highlands Inn, when my taste in men had significantly elevated.) On October 22, 1966, my new husband and I drove away after the ceremony in a light green '57 Chevy station wagon, dragging shoes and beer cans a couple of hours down the road to the Motel 6 near San Luis Obispo. We splurged on brunch at the Madonna Inn the next morning, its interior famously all copper and pink and velvety.

Just two weeks before our wedding, my high school dropout fiancé obtained his first job during the year I had known him. Until then, his mother would leave him a pack of Lucky Strikes and a dollar in an ashtray on the kitchen counter daily and a five-dollar bill on Fridays. He'd stuff the money into his shirt pocket once he woke up: just in time to grab a cup of coffee, pick me up from school at noon, and take me to work. Just in the nick of time—before becoming a husband—Dan became gainfully employed as a Chevron Standard gas station attendant, complete with white uniform shirt and pants and requisite hat and black belt. This was during the era when a young man pumped the gas, washed the windshield, and checked the oil, red rag in his back pocket as ubiquitous as a hanky in a gentleman's suit jacket— should a lady need one. Within a year or so, with the recommendation of a friend, he became a mechanic at an auto dealership.

After Dan and I were married, I got a full-time job with Pacific Bell as an information operator. With three local phone books in front of me, automated calls flew into my headset, my rubber-covered fingers flipping those pages to find the requested name, number, and address within the allotted seconds. After six months of minding all the rules and regulations, I quit to become a bank teller. Instead of sitting all day pelted by impatient 411 callers, now I was standing in heels on the cold cement floor of the bank dealing with often rude members of the public and their money. More rules and unreasonable expectations of employees who were, of course, all women. I met my job with a strong work ethic and the ability to follow rules, but I had my limits. A bank vice president introduced me to the experience of working with sexually inappropriate and entitled men and led me to quit my job six months later (#MeToo). I cried, sitting in my car in the parking lot, anticipating telling Dan I had quit my job, afraid of what he would do to me or the guy. Clearly that VP had no idea what a badass my husband was. I didn't tell Dan the truth. I didn't tell anyone that truth, certain I would be blamed for enticing my employer, knowing he would never take responsibility for his wandering hands and solicitations for sex. Never one to be unemployed for long, I soon secured a job back in health care.

On April 9, 1968, while home watching Martin Luther King Jr.'s funeral on TV, I received a phone call from Kaiser Hospital with the news that I had been hired. That same day, a man I had yet to meet also received a call from Kaiser and accepted a new job. Eddie Johnson was at home watching the funeral too. We started our new jobs on the same day and met during orientation. Eddie was handsome, charismatic, confident, twenty-eight, and Black. I was blond, cute, determined, nineteen, white, and married to Dan. Eddie had been pursuing a singing career—hoping for a Motown breakthrough—and carried himself with soul and style. Eddie and I became friends, and to my surprise, serious me got a little flirty.

I loved my new job and soon developed a whole new social circle that included people of color for the first time. Until then, my life was all white and mostly suburban. I had previously been exposed to African American culture through the maid at my grandmother's hotel, along with popular music, the Motown explosion, and television—all of which had a long way to go before they became truly representative. The diversity building in my life felt right and natural. As I made new friends and expanded my awareness and focus of concern away from that of my childhood, my heart began to drive me toward a lifelong engagement with racial justice that I couldn't have anticipated.

I continued my effort to be a "good wife," but my marriage to Dan was turning less tolerable, more untenable. I had no good counsel, direction, or loving advice and still felt as alone as ever in my personal life choices. Work became a safe, encouraging, and inspiring place. I received training, recognition, promotions, and opportunities to grow professionally. I felt strong, encircled by people who saw something in me, and I wasn't scared or demeaned there.

While I was still working at the bank, Dan and I had bought a small three-bedroom track house in Belmont. We had adopted a sweet German shepherd named Heidi who kept me company. I got my bouffant hair frosted as often as I could set the money aside to pay for it. I rarely bought new clothes but dressed

tastefully for work in matching skirts and sweaters and the required high heels and stockings. I thoroughly cleaned my house
and grocery shopped every Saturday, then late in the afternoon,
my girlfriend would arrive with her baby daughter after her chores
were complete and the two of us would make extravagant salami
sandwiches with lots of mayonnaise on French sourdough rolls. I
did the laundry, cooked the meals, washed the dishes, painted the
kitchen, pulled weeds, planted flowers, and picked up dog poop.
I secretly saved for a Mediterranean-style coffee table set I was
lusting after at Macy's, and often came home to find engines,
transmissions, and random pieces of the next hot rod littering the
front yard. Dan dropped his dirty laundry wherever it landed, argued about taking out the garbage for pickup, walked by raising
his hand like he might hit me, and twice pushed my face into the
dirty dishpan while I was washing dishes, just to be an ass. Shame-
lessly, during the one time he finally mowed the lawn, he accepted
the champagne the neighbors left for him on the porch. I picked
out names for our three prospective children and hoped for better
times ahead, all in the name of love.

Most of Dan's time outside of work was spent with buddies
fixing cars, cruising and racing those cars on the street or at the
drags, and sitting for hours in Mister Donut's coffee shop on El
Camino Real bullshitting about how fast they had been driving
when they outran the cops. Imagine how annoying they were to
the waitresses, those poor women just trying to make a living in
their aproned uniforms with stiff pin-on hankies, putting up with
the antics of these local hoodlums and their endless requests for
refills on the purchase of one cup of coffee each with no tip.

Aside from my cherished home, married life brought me little
joy, but my emotional state hadn't changed much from the year
before we were married. Perhaps I could have given my plans for

a husband and children a little more time and a lot more thought, or taken my parents up on their offer to attend the Sorbonne in Paris. "Take a little time away and after a year in college, if you still want to marry Dan, we'll support you." *No thanks!* Nothing in my upbringing had given me that level of confidence or trust.

While I was sitting home in baby doll pajamas trying to look sexy for my husband's arrival from his typical evening out, Dan's behavior had been growing more reckless and mean-spirited. He stayed out late, and when he returned, became increasingly belligerent and demanding. I began spending nights lying in bed, cuddled up to Heidi, envisioning a call from police saying Dan had been killed in an accident and thinking that his death marked the only way I would escape this mess—a call that would not have surprised me or many others, given his erratic life and driving habits.

In 1967, six months after Dan and I married, my mother and stepfather left the United States to move to someplace called Kathmandu in Nepal, a place I had never heard of until then. My stepfather had a new job with USAID (United States Agency for International Development). My sister and stepsister were deposited at the American School in New Delhi, India, for high school, and my youngest brother, Billy, then nine, accompanied our parents to Kathmandu.

As they were preparing to leave, my relationship with my mom had ironically become as good as it had ever been. I loved seeing her happy, with a sense of security, and new life adventure ahead. As a going-away gift, I presented her with a beautiful, heavy gold-linked charm bracelet with a single charm: a heart engraved with the date they were leaving, "May 5, 1967," on one side and "Love, Dan and Kris" on the other. She added charms to the bracelet as they traveled the world and she continued wearing it for many years.

When my marriage to Dan finally unraveled, my mother would ask me if I wanted her to remove the heart with Dan's name on it. "No, it doesn't bother me," I told her. Then, in an uncharacteristic show of thoughtfulness, she asked if I thought that keeping the heart charm might bother my then husband. Again, my answer was no. At that point, I didn't feel the need to erase my past, just move beyond it—and I had.

Divorcing One Idea of Love

After two and a half years of marriage, my 1969 divorce from Dan was as fiery as our former union. In the months leading up to our divorce, my brother Robert had come home from Vietnam and rented a cottage nearby. He'd become my confidant and fellow strategist. The timing was a problem, though, because as I screwed up my courage to leave Dan, my family was due home from their post in Kathmandu. Our parents were planning to stay with friends, but my sisters and brother Billy were due to stay at our house while on home leave. Everyone felt the tension once they arrived. While my husband lobbied my stepdad for support, I was talking with my mother about my plan to leave. It was only days before Dan and I faced the final blowup.

As Apollo 11 landed on the moon in July, I was sunning with girlfriends on the beach at Searsville Lake and listening to the collective excitement on everyone's transistor radio. That's when my husband chose to make his ill-timed arrival. "Oh, my God, Dan's here!" The face of my girlfriend Georgia, who'd spotted him first, paled through her sunburned cheeks. Red-faced and furious, Dan marched across the beach toward us with clenched fists. Reaching our blanket, he grabbed my purse, dumped its contents onto a towel, and proceeded to tear up every item containing my married name. This didn't amount to much in those days, since women weren't allowed to have a credit card or bank account in their own name. Still, pieces of my driver's license flew, then he tore the money from my wallet, scooped up my keys, and with a slap to the side of my head, stormed away, saying, "If you want a divorce, this is where it starts. I'm taking my name back."

My parents, sisters, and brothers were nervously waiting for me at home later when Georgia dropped me off. I heard the words: "Dan's home and he's really mad!" My family then walked around, packing up, and told me they thought it best that they leave and allow us to work things out. Once I was alone with Dan, I tried to be strategic, tentatively broaching the idea of a trial separation. As the conversation escalated, I switched tactics: "Okay, then, I want a divorce!" After beating me from one end of the house to the other, while I stood there with the earrings torn from my ears and the blouse ripped off my back, Dan slammed out the screen door, threatening to go kill my parents. He squealed out of our driveway in his truck, burning rubber down the street for a block. I called the friend's home where my parents were staying, hysterical, trying to alert them about Dan's words and intentions.

But Dan returned in about fifteen minutes, apparently unaware of where my family had gone. He popped open a beer can and watched me through narrowed eyes before tossing the can and its frothy contents at me. While I was mopping up the beer, my parents pulled into the driveway. I ran out to their car, hopped into the back seat, and let them drive me away. That would be the last time I saw my home, my dog, and most of my belongings, including the Mediterranean-style coffee table I'd saved up to buy. On the way out, my parents let me stop by a phone booth at a nearby gas station, and I called Dan's mother to let her know I was leaving. Never having shared with his parents just how abusive and damaged he was—although I'm pretty sure they knew—I thought I owed it to his mother to say goodbye. Dan had beaten me up, had thrown a full beer at me, was destroying our house, and was threatening to kill my parents—maybe Dan's mom and dad might want to go check on him. My mother-in-law begged me not to call the police. I didn't. I never spoke with Dan's parents again.

Recently, I googled Dan. I learned that he had died in 2010 and that his favorite job had been driving a truck for Neil Young's concert tours in the '70s or '80s—the timeline in the article was unclear. Based on the obituary, which didn't indicate a cause of death, I'm not sure much else happened for him. No wife or children were mentioned. Eleven people wrote condolences on the website. "RIP," most of them said. Then, "He was a good friend if you called after his first cup of coffee and if the news or NASCAR races weren't on." I'm guessing he would have been watching FOX News. What could I add? Thank you, Dan, for teaching me two things that have served me well:

1. How to drive a stick shift.

2. How to roll a joint.

And yes, thanks for setting the bar so low I could only go up after you. Rest in peace, Dan.

Love, Unexpected

Over the year preceding my divorce, as I introduced Dan to my new friends from work at Kaiser, his unveiled racism began seeping out. I had grown close to two of the female lab technicians I worked with, and together, we went from living the life we'd been raised to live to exploring aspects of the women we were destined to become. When one of them was moving out of state, I hosted her going-away party, and risky as it seemed, invited all of our friends from work—a group diverse in race, age, and gender.

The night of the party Dan sulked in a large wingback chair, beer in hand, legs stuck straight out into the living room, daring me to ask him to pull them in. His glare: a preview of the explosion gathering within. Eddie Johnson brought along his ex-wife Carolyn, the mother of four of his then-five children, his co-conspirator, and his cover date for the evening. Carolyn and Eddie sang a few songs as friends and colleagues moved to the rhythm of their soulful sound. The party turned out to be fun. We ate and drank, danced, and talked. Despite Dan's negative presence, people connected and had a good time. Recklessly, Eddie and I stole a kiss in the hallway.

"Be careful. He's watching you," cautioned a friend who'd spotted us.

I think Dan felt my synergy with Eddie, but he didn't know for sure. "What do you think the neighbors will say about your new friends?" Dan had the nerve to blurt out when we fought the next day. "You're not going to embarrass me like that."

I responded with, "How do you think they feel about you never mowing the lawn and leaving your car parts everywhere?"

And then our fight got worse. I was still learning when to keep my mouth shut with Dan, and he wasn't making it easy.

My life in 1969 was turning upside down and I felt guilty and scared. I also felt loved by a man for the first time. Dan was my first husband, but Eddie was my first love. Our love grew out of a friendship over coffee breaks and amid the whispers of other women in the hospital. Black women and white women had opinions about me. I was naive but purposefully oblivious to their thoughts and judgments. Eddie lit up the room when he walked in. When he beamed that smile on me, I lit up too. His confidence and what he called his "mother wit," his innate intelligence, and his street smarts only added to his charm. He wrote me love notes and boldly sent them through interoffice mail, pursuing me over lunch and during breaks in the hospital cafeteria. The man I fell in love with was warm and smart; he convinced me I was the love of his life.

After a year of friendship and flirtation with Eddie, I could barely stand my husband. I struggled to maintain a sense of balance as I observed the growing contrast between these two men in my life. Dan became increasingly hateful and abusive and did nothing toward the upkeep of our home and yard, our dog, and our life together. Unfortunately, the prevailing sentiment of the times and of my mother in particular was "You made your bed and now you have to sleep in it." I had been trying to lie in this bed I'd made, but going to work was a playful respite and becoming my favorite place to be. At work, I was acknowledged, appreciated, and more than good enough.

Trying to save my marriage—because it was the right thing to do—I looked for help. Therapy was not commonly available in the '60s, and without knowing who to turn to, I sought counsel from my gynecologist. I explained to him my marital misery over

Dan's abuse and our unsatisfying sex life and the challenges I was having trying to navigate or communicate my feelings. The doctor, a paunchy, white, sixty-something male, immediately escorted me out of the exam room, patting me on the shoulder as I went. "Oh, honey," he said, "your husband's probably just wearing orange socks and you'd rather he be wearing purple. It'll be okay. Just go home and give him some slack."

Seriously?

I did try talking with Dan about the absence of intimacy in our marriage and our inability to communicate about our sex life and our lack of sexual experience or awareness. I struggled to find the words, but I forced myself to give my marriage this chance. "Sounds like a personal problem," he replied. "Work it out the best way you can." I tried to work out this "personal problem," and then I actually found a way to do so—outside our marriage. I would leave Dan after innumerable humiliations, abuses, and threats. My mother promised to "never say I told you so, but . . ." and she reminded me again and again with pointed righteousness over my "mistakes." Once, with great sincerity, she said, "I thought you married Dan because he was so handsome." Incredulous, I laughed, saying, "You did? I never thought he was handsome!"

After my dramatic escape from Dan, I left town and then the country. I was afraid of Dan and didn't trust I would be safe getting an apartment on my own, keeping my job, and seeing Eddie—which definitely would have been my preference then. My parents were a big part of that exodus and had expressed their willingness, if not their compulsion, to take charge. I thought I had no other options. If I was divorced before my twenty-first birthday, I would be eligible to become a legal dependent of my parents once again and travel to live in Taipei with my mother, youngest brother, and stepsister, while my stepfather was stationed in Vietnam for USAID. Over the next few months, I let that plan roll forward.

I quit my job without notice, snuck in a quick goodbye to Eddie, and ran away with my two sisters and two of my brothers seeking refuge at Auntie Tina's home in Bellingham, Washington. We drove up and invaded the basement of her tiny one-bedroom dollhouse until our overseas travel began. Dan continued to troll around San Mateo throughout the summer, leaving notes on my parents' car window while they were eating at restaurants or visiting their friends' houses, begging them to help him get me back. Then, just as I was about to stop looking over my shoulder in fear, Dan called me one day from a motel in Bellingham. He'd found me. I spent hours on the phone with him as he alternately begged and threatened me. He placed a personal ad in *The Bellingham Herald*: "Little girl, your lion needs you. Please come home." He was referencing my childhood and the guardian lion statues in San Francisco's Sutro Heights Park. Connecting him to my childhood guardians and calling him "my lion" was the most sincere intimacy we had ever shared. Finally, I convinced Dan to go back home.

My family seemed oddly cohesive during that time. My parents bought me a new wardrobe and we began to look forward to our trip, which involved taking a freighter from Seattle to Yokohama, and then flying to Taipei. Once we arrived, we got settled into American compound housing, my mother hired a housekeeper, a driver, and a cook, and I began figuring out how to once again be a dependent of my parents.

With Ned in Vietnam, I treasured getting to know my mother as another adult woman. I was also in Taiwan to help with Billy and Cappy when my mother visited Ned in Vietnam every couple of months. Billy and Cappy were attending the American School in Taipei. I chased away cockroaches, explored the neighborhoods, learned to speak embarrassingly little Chinese, and played bridge with the neighbors in the afternoon. Intolerant of the driver my mother had hired, I got my Taiwanese driver's license and boldly headed into wild Taipei traffic in a white four-door 1965 Chevy Bel Air that my parents had shipped from the States. I took college classes at the University of Maryland extension campus and made friends with American military wives safe-havened in Taiwan while their husbands were in Vietnam.

I met a physical therapist who was married to an army officer stationed in Vietnam and helped her to start a volunteer program at a Chinese children's rehabilitation center. There, we engaged the American wives to work with the kids on craft projects and provide English lessons between therapy sessions. It was a fulfilling effort, especially so when we arranged a visit from the television actor Raymond Burr of *Ironside* fame, previously known for his defense lawyer role in *Perry Mason*. We were thrilled with his donation of two wheelchairs. Volunteering gave the military wives something else to do while their kids were in school besides sitting at the bar in the officers' club drinking twenty-five-cent scotch. All the rest was covered, since everyone had maids, nannies, and cooks.

In the end, I'd had a good year abroad, but I was ready to go home and retrieve my independence. Robert was attending the University of Denver and Barb would be heading there for her second year in college. Now that I'd learned to once again accept an overload of parental involvement, I enrolled there too. Robert was on the GI Bill, but the parents paid Barb's and my tuition and living expenses, including the apartment Barb and I shared. I wasn't back on my own yet.

On my return from Taiwan in August 1970, I stopped for a few weeks in San Francisco to see friends and family. The day before I was to leave for college in Denver, I called Eddie. We spent the night together. We exchanged letters and calls from Denver for a while, until I received a letter from the woman—as it turned out—he had been living with for years. This was not the first or the last of the reasons Eddie would give me to leave him in the rearview.

No Love for Denver

Denver was not for me. I arrived at the end of August 1970 in eighty-degree weather. Then on Labor Day weekend, it snowed. In their promotional pitches, people who loved it there exclaimed over the state's magnificent mountains, the hiking, and the skiing, but if you're an ocean person like me, the mountains fall flat. And snow in the middle of a heat spell? One day on the bus to my part-time job in winter, I sat behind an older couple. "Fred, look," a woman exclaimed to her husband as the bus drove by a guy walking with chin-length hair and a jean jacket. "There's a hippie!" So archaic. And again, so not for me.

After just two quarters at Denver University, I moved back to San Francisco in May 1971 exuding happiness as I strolled down Market Street. From one employment agency to the next, I smiled when a real hippie handed me a flower on one corner and laughed when construction workers whistled at me on the next. I loved being back in the City by the Bay, where people seemed so authentic and accepting. The fog rolled in daily, keeping some neighborhoods cool, but with just a short ride over a hill I could be in the sun in ten minutes and at the beach day or night for fun or solitude. I was home!

I got a job in an internal medicine office at 909 Hyde Street and an apartment on 25th and Geary and began my San Francisco life with a return trip to divorce court. After I was granted a divorce in court before leaving for Taiwan, Dan had prevented our divorce from becoming final through some technicality that enabled him to contest the original decree. We both showed up in court dressed for show after not seeing or speaking to each other for about two years. He wore a beard, jeans, a suede, sheepskin-lined vest, and expensive cowboy boots. I wore a rust-colored knit mini dress with a snakeskin belt at my hips and matching handmade snake plat- form sandals from Taipei: fabulous and ridiculously cheap.

After the judge granted and gaveled our divorce into being, Dan and I went to lunch, smoked a joint, and hung out for a few months. It seemed he had mellowed out—but not really. Once again, he wasn't working, so most days he picked me up after work. Passing me the joint in the truck, we'd head back to my apartment, I'd change out of my uniform, and we'd go out to dinner. He had just sold our house in Belmont and had money but no inclination to give any of it to me. Soon I was bored, unconvinced about a future together, and ready to get back on my own path. I refused the cross-country road trip he wanted to take us on and we broke up in a much more civilized way than we had previously. I carried on with my life and my friends in San Francisco.

I loved working. My early jobs gave me opportunities to learn higher levels of responsibility and develop technical, clinical, and administrative skills—and to grow personally. One instance of personal growth involved my ability to take a stand for myself. My friend Carrie, who shared the front desk with me at the med- ical office, had announced she was getting married, and I knew she would be leaving the practice soon. The day Dr. M came out of his office throwing a full-blown red-faced tantrum as well as a twelve-inch stack of patient charts in our direction, I told Carrie I would be taking the next day off to find a new job. The reason for the doctor's fury? The pink, handwritten phone message paper-clipped to the front of one of the charts had attached itself to the back of the chart on top. Dr. M had a chart without a message on the front. What was he to do?

I gave my notice that Friday and started working at Children's Hospital in San Francisco. I started as a lab assistant, was promoted to supervisor of central processing, trained as an EKG technician, and then secured my last job at Children's as a unit clerk on the maternity floor. I loved moving around and learning. Again, I developed a solid sense of confidence in my working life.

The training and job growth was great, but best of all were the lifelong friends I made while working at the hospital, including Marilyn, an EEG tech; Lu, an ob-gyn ultrasound tech; and Eleanor, a respiratory therapist. In 1978, I met Cynthia when she started working at St. Mary's Medical Center in radiation oncology. By that time I was doing the professional billing for the doctors' radiation oncology corporation and traveling around to see patients in four San Francisco hospitals. That was roughly when Marilyn met Andee, a hairstylist a year ahead of me in high school and Lu met Colleen at the elementary school where their children were schoolmates. The seven of us—Marilyn, Lu, Eleanor, Cynthia, Andee, Colleen, and I—would go on to be longtime sisters, supporters, and family. We would expand our circle many times through the years, but our crew of seven remained the core.

When our group of seven met, we were mostly one "was-band" (read "ex-husband") into womanhood and still in our early twenties. I was the only one without children, but as children came along for me, these women became their aunties for life. We lived the best years anyone ever could in San Francisco, the '70s into the '80s. Our hospital stories, capers, and escapades were reckless, fabulous, and sworn to secrecy. As each of us went on to acquire one or two more husbands, we successively elevated our good judgment and taste in men, expanded our careers, raised our children, and supported and loved one another through the challenges and blessings we faced—true to this day.

ACT III

Love, Racism, and Pain

Eddie Johnson often crossed my mind. We hadn't spoken in maybe a year and a half since I had received that letter from the woman he lived with. One day I left work at Children's early, went home, showered, dressed, and drove to Kaiser Hospital, where he still worked. I walked into the pathology lab where he was a histology technician and diener (autopsy technician). Startled, he stared. "Give me a minute," he said. He pulled off his lab coat, grabbed his jacket, and said, "Let's go." And that was it. Eddie followed me back to the city, we went out for dinner, he came back to my apartment, and our reunion was magical. I knew I loved Eddie Johnson and he loved me. Former red flags be damned!

Eddie introduced me to a new world more alive and real than anything I had known. A world where truth and lies were called out at the kitchen table, everyone's "business" and indiscretions became open for conversation if not a joke, rich stories and old times were shared, anger was on display as unresolved grudges erupted, differences of opinion were shouted, alcohol was poured and guns were fired into the air on New Year's Eve. I felt alive, uncomfortable, and then horrified when I became the object of the joke one night at the dinner table after Eddie revealed a fight had taken place between us. (An unthinkable admission in my family.) Family, in Eddie's world, was tight and love was deep and visceral. No one said things were "fine" when they weren't. Ultimately, I became a part of his family with all its love, complexities, and differences. Eddie and I married on April 14, 1973, five years after we had met.

Eddie was a man who could get things done and he loved planning the wedding and the after party. We had a sweet, rather traditional wedding with family and friends at a Lutheran church Eddie had found. We had never attended services there but went to meet with the pastor who was happy to preside. Eddie and his best man, Andrew, wore gray tuxedos that they'd picked out and kept secret. I wore a long, empire waist "hippie-style" dress Barb had made. Actually, she had been making it for herself, but I told her I loved the large yellow-and-navy floral print, prompting her to give it to me for a wedding dress. Wearing a light blue floor-length dress, Barb was my maid of honor. Robert walked me down the aisle, though I was touched when Dr. Cosgrove—the pathologist Eddie worked with at Kaiser—initially offered to do the honors.

Life married to Eddie was a roller-coaster ride. The highs and lows, the best and the worst. At the beginning of our tumultuous ride, we agreed that whenever we argued, we would never threaten to leave. We loved each other and were committed to working on our relationship. Our union would never be easy, but our highs were the best, and the rest of the time, I worked hard to understand the source of our conflicts. Adding to our personal challenges were the societal pressures of being an interracial couple. San Francisco politics, the "Zebra killers," the kidnapping of Patty Hearst, and the terrorist antics of the Symbionese Liberation Army had the city on edge, and local police detained my Black husband on his way home from work with some regularity.

I found these events frightening, the beginning of my education about the dysfunctional dynamic between African Americans and police. On the flip side, our friends, jobs, family, the music scene, jazz clubs—all the good things about living in San Francisco— kept us distracted or entertained.

Once again, my parents were not thrilled by my marriage. But they were stationed in Vietnam, giving them little influence over me—aside from an occasional upsetting letter. They did, however, forbid Billy from coming to my home. Dutiful to our parental training, Billy, Barb, Robert, and I obeyed their instructions—for a while.

I loved the magical, mystical activity always brewing beneath the surface of my life, and in this case, it seemed like the great cosmos had a hand in bringing my family together. Eddie often commuted to work on the Greyhound bus from San Francisco to Redwood City. Billy was in boarding school in nearby Menlo Park since Mom had decided to go to live in Vietnam with Ned. One Friday evening, Billy was taking the bus to San Francisco to spend the weekend with Barb and Robert, who had also moved back from Denver. Eddie got on the bus and sat right down beside Billy. They soon realized their connection and we all took it from there. Billy loved Eddie and Eddie loved Billy. As a result, while we were all living in San Francisco, Barb, Robert, Billy, Eddie, and I took a step in the direction of our own truths. The parents had to make their adjustments on their next trip home. "As hard as I fought to keep you apart," Ned told Eddie, "I'll fight that hard to keep you together." I believed him at the time and my heart soared with hope for my family.

I learned many adulting behaviors and skills with Eddie, from paying bills and budgeting to sexual intimacy and body awareness to racism, Black culture and history, drinking, and multiple ways to experience heartache—most of which were previewed and for-given again and again.

In contrast to all the reasons to leave or put a halt to my rela-tionship with Eddie, our daughter, Holly, was the reason I believe we were compelled, if not destined, to be together. I believe that before we incarnate or are born into this physical life, we make agreements with other souls. These agreements are in support of our spiritual growth in this lifetime and are often referred to as "soul contracts." I believe Holly chose to come into this life through us. All I had ever really wanted was to be loved, to love, and to be someone's mother, and she was the most beautiful ful-fillment I could have imagined. I loved her immediately and forever. Holly would become a huge influence in the direction of my growth and inquiry. She would continue to remind me of the love Eddie and I shared, as well as the blessings, heartaches, and responsibilities I have been given and said yes to in my life.

Holly was born in Seattle. We had been ecstatic about being pregnant and after a year of marriage, Eddie and I had moved to Seattle on an adventure to see what our life would be like away from family and friends—and Eddie's exes, thank you! With Holly's birth, our love burst from us more fully than ever. Just looking at her took our breath away. A new experience and a fresh start together as a family. And the beginning of my spir-itual awakening—having been without faith since the death of my father.

But Seattle, it turned out, wasn't having us. Seattle was far more openly racist and intolerant of our interracial presence than San Francisco had ever been. With my belly growing during preg-nancy and my long, blond hair and dark-skinned husband, we stood out. We would be stared at, ridiculed, angered, and embar-rassed. During a job interview at a Seattle hospital, Eddie was told to "go back to California; we don't want you here." Not a bad idea, perhaps, since the job he was applying for in pathology paid half of what he had made in California. He ended up accepting a position at an electrical supply company as a warehouseman, where he was the first person of color ever hired. We were told that management had met with all the employees to be sure they could work with a Black person. (I can't confirm the language actually used, but I'm suspicious, given that these folks Eddie worked with had talked about their weekend sport of "taking pot shots at the Indians who were fishing on the river.") Eddie and I turned those people into friends for the time we stayed. They gave us a baby shower and a blue onesie with a hand-sewn "32" on the front and "Little O. J." on the back—an acknowledgment of the superstar football player and Eddie's favorite at the time—well before O. J. Simpson's infamous fall from grace.

One evening, dressed up in a soft pink maternity outfit, six months pregnant, and out for dinner with my tall, dark, and handsome husband, we had strolled hand in hand into a lovely waterfront restaurant on Lake Washington. Seated near a window, admiring the boats docked below, I was attempting to cut the small, round loaf of warm sourdough that arrived on a breadboard with a serrated knife. Without warning, my hand slipped, and the ramekin of whipped butter flew off the table, splashing onto the floor and apparently a woman's leg under a nearby table. Embarrassing under any circumstance. And then the woman stood up and began screaming the unspeakable N-word, and calling me a "clumsy, N-loving whore." So was our life in Seattle in 1974.

At home in our partially furnished apartment, we'd listen to music—our records, stereo, and television being the bulkiest items we'd had room for in our Pinto during our move to Seattle. Often on weekends while we were up through the night nursing

Holly, Eddie would spend the time explaining his basketball plays and strategy for the upcoming game. He had started coaching a little league basketball team and was also helping a guy he'd met coach a Little League football team. *So much fun,* I thought then, *and great for building a new community in our lives.* That year Eddie won the leagues' Basketball Coach of the Year award, though his tough, untalented little team lost every game.

We stayed in Seattle for sixteen months, enduring thanks to supportive family: my aunts and cousins who lived in Seattle and Bellingham and Eddie's aunts and uncle living in Portland. They were loving and always made us feel welcome. We went in one direction or the other as often as we could, grateful for family and a rest from the pressure of racism and our aloneness in Seattle. We suffered behind our smiles, however, while the inescapable racism took its toll.

Love Disappoints

The First Slap

In a world where a man's rage, disguised as love,
    seduces a young and unsuspecting woman's heart
    then slaps her silly, how would a girl ever find her way to
    Dreamland?
No one told her the Prince was wounded with a wandering eye
    or that his body would never be faithful,
    even as his mouth said, "You're the one, the only one."
Dreamily, she believed him. Until . . .

The first slap knocked the light out of her love.

The first slap that previewed more to come but is never believed in Dreamland.

The first slap that made me flinch for the rest of my life.

The first slap that let me know there was trouble in paradise.

The first slap that said, "Leave and never go back."

The first slap few women listen to but forever wish they had.

The first slap and the apology that echoed in the emptiness of my broken heart but didn't give me the courage to say goodbye.

The first slap that had me thinking I could love him into being a better man.

The first slap that straightened my spine and built the first layer of a shell around my heart, a shell that grew solid and that even the last slap couldn't shatter.

One summer weekend in 1975, I flew with eight-month-old Holly to San Francisco for a visit and to explore ways to move home. In those days, finding a job could be as easy for me as opening the phone book to the listing on "hospitals" in the yellow pages. I interviewed for a job as a unit clerk on the oncology floor at Saint Francis Memorial Hospital and was hired the same day. I flew back to Seattle with Holly and packed our clothes to return and start my new job on the Tuesday after Labor Day. Eddie stayed in Seattle for another two months and four paychecks to make the last two payments on our car. He drove home to San Francisco and arrived looking thin and tired.

Eddie's parents owned a Victorian in the Western Addition neighborhood on Fulton Street. When the tenants moved out of the first-floor flat, Eddie and I moved in, paid the rent, and made it our home. His parents lived in the second-floor flat, and his sister Ruth and her two sons lived on the third floor. Eddie arranged for babysitting for Holly with Mrs. Roberts, a well-loved older woman across the street. I was grateful for her and for the convenience. Everything was falling into place. We were family and happy to be back in San Francisco, starting over.

I loved my new job. Claudia, the progressive head nurse who hired me, gave me the creative freedom to develop my position beyond the typical expectations of a clerical position. It would now include the care of patients and families. I took courses in cancer counseling and was dedicated to learning as much as I could in support of my growing opportunity to serve. In addition to facilitating communication on the tenth floor cancer ward, transcribing and placing doctors' orders, and answering phones and questions from anyone who stepped off the elevator, I made daily rounds and added patient and family advocate and ombudsman to my job description. I was an administrative manager, hostess, problem-solver, friend, empath, resource, and messenger for many. I was beginning to know more about myself and what made me come alive.

I became interested in the political changes in medicine and health care delivery and holistic health modalities. With Claudia's introduction, I avidly experimented with visualization for pain management based on the early work of oncologist Dr. Carl Simonton and other cancer innovators and I actively supported my nurse friends with their groundbreaking startup, Nurses In Transition. It was during that time that I learned to meditate, then to hold space and be a quiet presence for the dying. I would discover that cancer awakens us to many things, and I was an eager and sensitive student to these teachings. Gaining professional perspective and direction, I worked enthusiastically, made new friends, and with my baby and husband, got resettled in San Francisco. Life was good.

It was easy to explain Eddie's weight loss when he arrived home. I'd been in California for two months without him and perhaps he hadn't eaten properly on his own, or maybe it was the stress of being in Seattle, or how he'd spent his time in my absence. Endless possibilities, though he had little energy and soon seemed to be getting sick. Possibly a cold, or just a cough—the diagnostic chest X-rays had been negative—but he continued to lose weight.

Six months into my cancer immersion on the tenth floor and just weeks from his thirty-sixth birthday, Eddie was diagnosed with lung cancer. Nothing had prepared me for this. Not my training, eagerness to learn, the tenderness of patients, or the support of my coworkers. I was devastated. Fear of his cancer diagnosis ran through my body in waves of nausea. Always the question "Why?" hovered, and I was scared. Scared of what medical horrors we were facing. Scared to lose him. Scared for Holly to lose her Daddy. Having learned compassion from being in service to other cancer patients, I couldn't find it for myself and had no idea how to make the nightmare stop. It had never occurred to me that this was what I had been preparing for. Here I was, the young wife whose husband was just given a seeming death sentence.

Eddie endured horrific pain: a bronchoscopy to define the disease that led to the removal of his right lung and radiation therapy and other invasive surgeries and procedures from the time of his diagnosis in March throughout 1976. Imaging and diagnostics being what they were back then, the doctors really had no idea what was going on with the cancer inside Eddie's body. They kept trying to follow the pain patterns, attempting to give him relief. Eddie died February 1, 1977, after another failed surgery for pain management. The neurosurgeon who had planned to surgically interrupt the pain sensors in Eddie's brain stem reappeared too quickly that morning after Eddie was taken to the operating room. "I couldn't do the surgery," he announced to my surprised face in a clipped, irritated tone. I felt a sudden chill. "He has pneumonia."

When I asked when we could take Eddie home, the surgeon refused to discharge him. "If I let you take him home," he told me, "it will be considered a clear case of euthanasia."

I was stunned by the doctor's blatant insensitivity, but truthfully, I had considered the prospect of putting Eddie out of his misery. During the long months of caring for Eddie at home, administering a cache of narcotics and numerous other drugs, day and night, I had considered euthanasia as a humane escape for him and suicide as freedom from this nightmare for myself. But as I considered the end of Eddie's life and mine, my reason to live was clear. I chose to live only because I didn't trust anyone to explain to Holly in my absence how much I loved her. That is the strength of the love that bound me, and still binds me, to my daughter.

I had considered suicide as a teen and had written about it in English class in my junior year of high school, the only class in which I routinely did my written assignments. The assignment involved writing five pages each week in any format about any topic we wanted. The teacher would then talk about the papers anonymously in class—about the topics, not the punctuation. She created a "safe space," a term unknown to me at the time, and she used it skillfully to guide our young and sometimes frightened minds into more open spaces of acceptance than perhaps our families could offer. Her brother had committed suicide, and her wisdom and personal experience helped me explore my thoughts further. It was more of a pause than a resolution, though, as the prospect of an escape through death would linger in me for much of my life.

The care and attention I gave my husband came from a hundred percent of my love and from putting one foot in front of the other. The last few hours of his life he was communicative, ate a little broth and Jell-O, and miraculously experienced no pain for the first time in over a year. I sat with him tearfully as he left behind his scarred, emaciated, exhausted body.

It was important to Eddie that we have the money to cover his funeral, and somehow we saved what we needed and were especially grateful for the discount we received from funeral director Mr. Coleman. Coleman Funeral Home on Eddy Street happened to be next door to the first home Eddie's parents were able to buy to move their family out of the projects. Eddie had grown up helping Mr. Coleman and had developed a comfortable relationship with dead bodies as a result. These skills had later become helpful when Dr. Cosgrove offered Eddie training and a position in the pathology lab as a histology tech and diener at Kaiser Hospital.

Before becoming a part of Eddie's family, the only funeral I had ever attended was my father's closed casket funeral—closed because of the trauma involved in his death. (I don't know, however, if under different circumstances my mother would have chosen an open casket.) When Eddie died, his sister Ruth took over most of the funeral arrangements. We picked out the casket together, but I was heartbroken and clueless when it came to executing a funeral befitting tradition and the way things were done in his family. More importantly, interfering just wasn't my way, and I really had no opinion or experience with the care or interment of a body after death. Ruth went right into action, and I was okay with that. I appreciated her taking charge.

My mother-in-law had died six months earlier, so I knew more or less what to expect at the funeral, the open casket not being the least of it. The AME Church, soulful spirituals, black limousines, flower wreaths, some heart-shaped and draped with banners: LOVING SON, LOVING BROTHER, LOVING FATHER, LOVING HUSBAND—more of those damn gladiolas and everyone back to the house for a delicious feast cooked by my sister-in-law and a few other family members. One of Eddie's teenage daughters was carried out screaming over the heads of several ushers, fans and tissues were waved, music played, and then came wailing and so much love. In addition to the tragedy of Eddie dying young, he had many friends and was loved and admired. The church and the house swelled to capacity and I was embraced by everyone there. I remained close to Eddie's family and to this day, I have a loving relationship with his children, his brother, and the few still alive to remember our days around the kitchen table listening to the elders meddle and tell their tales.

My one quiet moment occurred the day before the funeral in the late afternoon. I took our two-year-old daughter by myself to the funeral home where the "viewing" was expected to take place later that evening. I held Holly in my arms and cried looking at Eddie in the coffin, dressed in the smartly tailored gray suit he had purchased for his mother's funeral and worn to my brother Robert's wedding just two months earlier. Others would say, "He looked good!" "They did a good job!" I don't know about that. I said goodbye that afternoon alone with Holly. My way: personal, slow, and quiet.

It's impossible to measure the impact Eddie Johnson had and continues to have on my life. He changed the trajectory of my life and the things that concern and interest me. With him, I stepped into a life outside my childhood frame of reference, one I couldn't have imagined. I think of him. I've called on his strengths and cursed his weaknesses. I fell in love with a Black man, and it changed me.

Years after Eddie, I would go on to explore somatic writing— a form of writing that taps into emotions and memories held in the physical body—prompting the following poems to emerge. This poem speaks to a long-held belief in fairy-tale love and the permanent shattering of such illusions.

Someone I Loved

Someone I loved hit me.
He slapped my face when I wanted to drive because he was
    drunk.
I cried looking out the window while he drove.

Someone I loved hit me.
He shoved me aside and walked out the door, dressed to kill.
His friend watched and left me on the floor crying.

Someone I loved hit me.
Leaving me for hours or sometimes days, having taken our
    money from my jewelry box,
Calling through the night with apologies and promises.

Someone I loved hit me.
Came home drunk and raped me.
I never spoke of it, but I always knew.

Someone I loved hit me
    with the news that I had gonorrhea.
I sat with my baby on my lap in the county health department,
    shame radiating as I tried to hide from myself.

Someone I loved was hit with cancer.
I cared for him with all my love
    and tried to forget the worst of it.

Someone I loved died
    before becoming a better man.
I hid my shame with a smile and wore rose-colored glasses.

I never saw my father hit my mother, though hiding conflict is common among women abused by their mates. But as a child, it was obvious to me who had the power and the freedom. My father came home when he chose, hung out after work to drink if he chose, and had relationships with other women as he chose. As a young girl, I was keenly aware that men had the power and that women during the 1950s and '60s were publicly subservient and personally powerless, if not miserable. I signed right up!

I believed in fairy tales and happy endings, and I was willing to do the hard work required of Cinderella, but I definitely wanted the Prince.

With magnetic force he drew me to him, later to repel me as magnets and princes do. I only wanted to see the love, and when it was good, it was the best I had known.

Even the Poet Feels Rage

Before I was a poet, I was an abused wife.

Before I was a writer, I was an abused wife.

Before I had a child, a career or a college degree, I was an
    abused wife.

Before I was an abused wife, I was a girl constricted by the de-
    mands of strict parents, misused societal power, and my
    mother's admonition that you had to "suffer to be beautiful."

I accepted what came.

Perhaps I could write the memories away in a poem,
    describe only beauty and bouquets till death do us part.

But poems require truth and details.

Details of abuse left in the haze of shame.

I let the time of abuse tear quietly at my heart,
    thinking I cried only for his death
    and the cancer that took our life away.

As I unravel my grief,

I see that it has included the whole of Eddie.

And the broken parts of me.

Violence is a thief and, for a time, it stole the vision of beauty I had for my future. But beauty is a part of me. It connects me to myself, to others, and to nature. Beauty remains an anchor for me, unsullied by my mother's threats that I had to "suffer to be beautiful" or the violence used to control me when I was a young woman. Resilience is my superpower and beauty is essential to my life.

Awakening to my healing, I grieved, remembering the whole of Eddie, the whole of us. It's not the first time I've acknowledged the reality of his abuse, it's just deeper now and more pertinent to my healing heart. In this hateful world, I have felt protective of Eddie, not wanting him or any other Black man judged even more harshly because of the ways he had been shaped and behaved as a young man. For the most part, I kept this abuse to myself. Now I don't think anyone needs to be protected by my silence. Before I was loved by a man who never raised his hand and barely raised his voice in anger, I was an abused wife: truth.

In *Notes from Heaven*, authored by my brother Robert Frandeen, the angel reminds us that "the heat of Love is so strong that on Earth, Love must always be tempered by mercy and wisdom." As I bow to the altar of my life and explore this deeper form of earthly love, I am grateful for the wisdom and mercy that's accompanied this journey and the self-respect I've developed along the way.

Love Shifts Perspective

On Abuse of Women

On behalf of the young woman I was, I didn't cave under my sorrow. I didn't whimper in victimhood. I looked good, and like many abused women, I carried on with a lifetime of family, friends, adventure, education, exploration, love, and the painful secret of being subjected to violence, a secret I held in silence.

I married two men who were abusive. This fact is neither the whole of me, nor does it speak to the entirety of my experience with my first two husbands, my intelligence, or my capacity for love. I had yet to learn from Maya Angelou that when someone shows you who they are, believe them, or that when we know better, we are obliged to do better.

Abuse is part of what happened during my early years in relationships. Being the recipient of physical and emotional abuse diminished my capacity for trust and openness with others. These experiences color my thoughts today as I continue life's healing journey. Being a survivor of domestic abuse doesn't render my life good or bad or confine me to victimhood or make my husbands into monsters. I divorced my first husband before I was twenty-one and gratefully moved on—without children or other considerations—to love again. I left Dan with his anger, my car, the dog, and our house, along with most of the possessions in it. I was the "perfect ex-wife," according to some. My second husband, Eddie, died of lung cancer when he was thirty-six and I was twenty-eight. I do not cover for or protect him with my love any longer. And I do not accept the suggestion that I was wrong to love him or that his behavior suggests he didn't love me; he did. We were who we were—challengers and products of the times and the culture into which we were born.

It does hurt to feel the longing and heartache my sweet, fierce, younger self endured. I understand my choices and I've worked it out for myself, sufficient for this life. Sufficient, that is, until a new layer appears: a perspective of change or someone whose story draws me even deeper. I will attend to what comes as I always have. That is my nature.

I bow to the altar of my life to forgive myself for allowing my first two husbands to abuse me. I have learned that the abuse was not my fault, and that abuse is not allowed, it is endured. These ideas reflect the long distance I had to travel to get to that understanding. Much has been written about the problem of domestic violence. I have no simple answers or trite solutions to add. Who and why we love can be complicated. I have done my work to find resolution and peace within myself and to cultivate strength and the absolute knowledge that I could never and would never live under that kind of control again. I know better, so I've done better. I have also been blessed since then to experience love in a third marriage without violence or abuse of any kind. For that, I am grateful.

On Racism

A harsh imprint had been planted in my psyche as a young girl. It went like this: White women who are with Black men are fat, unattractive, low-class, and unable to get a white man. They are whores and get what they deserve. While driving up Sutter Street in San Francisco, my father made a derogatory comment to that effect as we drove past a white woman and Black man standing together on a corner, holding hands, waiting to cross the street. I heard my father's words before I even knew of a difference or that skin color mattered to people. I may have been eight or nine when my father made that remark, but it lodged in me like a bullet. A lesser legacy left by my dad.

I'm grateful for the lens through which I understand our human connection now and am deeply saddened by the separation and racism that continues to plague the United States. The 2008 election of Barack Obama as president was an unexpected and generous event. I am grateful I lived to see it, this most healing experience for me. The repercussions of that shift, however, have been devastating.

The murder of Black men and women at the hands of police and the repeated acquittal of white privilege, ignorance, and carefully cultivated fear continues to anger and hurt me. This is only news now to people who have never known Black people or people of color. I got an education when I met Eddie. He gave me the history lesson and the real-time experience in which I have lived, studied, and despaired for over fifty years now.

The atrocity of racism fills libraries. Those books illuminate and educate while society's behaviors continue to threaten the truth of how people of color in the United States experience the world. My witnessing of this struggle has been expansive, resulting in extraordinary heartache and disappointment. The reality of the struggle remains a threat to my children, my family, people I love, and society overall.

If I reflect on all of the study, spiritual inquiry, and healing work I have done across my lifetime, one thing I know for sure is that anything that causes separation is against our true nature, which is to love.

On Money

I wasn't taught how to navigate the world. I observed the behavior of adults, but no one ever talked with me about how to actually get things done. As a high school freshman, I learned how to type in one semester of class but couldn't begin to fathom shorthand. Hence, I squandered any potential I might have had for a career as an executive secretary. In home economics, I made an apron and a Baked Alaska. No help, there. I was usually above the allowed weight and didn't think I was pretty enough to become a flight attendant, and I had no desire to become a teacher. My mother, the registered nurse, told me I'd better "have something to fall back on" when I talked about my interest in interior design.

I learned some practical financial basics from Eddie, like how to list our pay dates on a tablet, subtract the rent, insurance, car payments and utility bills, estimates for food and gas, and set aside any leftover money toward a goal. That's how we saved to buy our first car together, a brand new, 1972, four-speed silver Ford Pinto that ran with no major repairs until 1987. We usually had a six-month running tablet keeping us on track. That scheme worked unless Eddie used our savings on a binge, followed by "I'm so sorry, I promise . . ." presents.

Money was a secret in my family and I guess in most families at that time. We followed what we were taught—that discussing or asking about money was impolite—which only added to my confusion when my parents fought over money. My sister and I had been playing outside one day when we were suddenly told to get into the car to take Daddy to the airport. He was heading off on another business trip or rendezvous, and I was crushed to hear him say, "Jesus, Bernice, can't you do something about those kids? They look like ragamuffins!" Maybe if they could have talked about money, my dad wouldn't have berated my mom while placing his bags in the trunk of the car. While sitting in the backseat of the car, all I could do was look down at my little striped T-shirt and jeans with rolled-up cuffs, showing dusty white socks and scuffed saddle shoes. I must have made a mental note about the importance of dressing nicely around men—no matter what the circumstances.

As kids, we thought my grandmother was rich. Did you get rich by driving a Cadillac and giving your grandchildren hand-me-downs for gifts? Maybe rich looked like the friends with the ski boat named *Pinky* and the big house in Hillsborough, and probably the people with weekend houses at Lake Tahoe. Our neighbors, who lived a few doors down from us on Parrott Drive, had a great-aunt Winnie, who occasionally dropped by from her mansion in Woodside. She made a grand arrival to our suburban neighborhood in her black limousine, driven by Bill, her Black, uniformed chauffeur. For sure, she was rich. I was afraid of her and everyone else seemed to be too.

Other than these early impressions, and besides getting a job and a paycheck, I knew nothing about money—and nobody was telling. The only way I thought I could get more money was to get a bigger paycheck. That was pretty much the ethos I would stand by for life. I got an education and a job with a title that paid well enough for me to do much of what I wanted for my kids and my home. Never enough to feel financially free, never with a thought for the future: just enough for plenty of food, good wine and entertainment, a nice car, family vacations, education and personal growth workshops, books, and a home that I loved.

While rolling through my savings during a time of creative bravery and entrepreneurial spirit, I consulted a financial advisor who specialized in working with women entrepreneurs. The sign on her door read A MAN IS NOT A FINANCIAL PLAN. Got it!

Working on Love after Eddie

I returned to my job at St. Francis Memorial Hospital a couple of months after Eddie died, once Holly and I had moved and settled into a beautiful old apartment in the Haight-Ashbury district. I had some adjusting to do. Not the least of which was leaving my washer and dryer behind and doing our laundry at a laundromat. Parking in the neighborhood was even more of a nightmare—carrying a two-year-old child sometimes blocks—and if I came home on a Saturday night and got the spot on the corner with the fire hydrant, I counted myself lucky. I would race the meter maids in the morning to relocate my car before getting a parking ticket I couldn't afford. Holly returned to day care at our babysitter Mrs. Roberts's home and began preschool at the Happy Day Christian School. New friends and new opportunities welcomed me back to work.

I was doing my best, but grief and tears hovered. I felt vulnerable, confident only in my care for Holly and through the support of my friends. Then I met Stephen Levine. Stephen, a poet and spiritual author, had been working on a project with Elisabeth Kübler-Ross, a pioneer in the study of the terminally ill and grief and the author of *On Death and Dying*. My friend Sister Patrice Burns invited Stephen to spend time with dying patients at the hospital's oncology unit. Sr. Patrice (affectionately known to many at the hospital as Patsy) made the introduction with a twinkle in her eye, and Stephen came over for dinner soon after. He brought my daughter a stuffed zebra. Stephen helped me to say goodbye to my late husband, and with time and his wisdom, I put my wedding photos away and moved back into life—a life that now included a meditation teacher and an expert on death and dying.

In the beginning of our friendship, I was out of my body and out of my mind. Stephen's warm soup and Sunday conversations at his house in Santa Cruz made for a gentle place to sit still, if only for a moment. Stephen gave me a signed copy of his first book, *Grist for the Mill*, written with beloved spiritual guru Ram Dass, and over the years I collected all of his newly published books. Stephen was a teacher to many, and I felt blessed to know him.

Back at work, however, I was surrounded by pain, cancer, and constant reminders—both of Eddie and of life's struggles and losses. I practiced meditation and life as a single mother and began socializing with friends and family again. These encounters could be surprisingly intense. The neighbors renting the entire third floor in my apartment building were friendly drug dealers (of weed, to my knowledge, but my ignorance was either bliss or blind). Gorgeous, antique furniture and rapturous sunlight filtered through voluptuous ferns in macrame-and-shell plant hangers. We became friendly with the dealers over hot tea and their warm company. Life got exciting a few months later with gunshots and police banging at the door late one night. I flushed a ten-dollar lid before answering the door. A waste, given that the police were looking for someone they thought might be in our backyard but wasn't.

Not long after the police incident, Holly and I came home one evening at dusk before the hall lights had been turned on. Halfway down the hall while heading toward our first-floor apartment, I noticed large pieces of splintered wood on the floor near the apartment where our neighbor Kean lived. As I tentatively approached his door, I saw that it was open, and through that inch I peeked, afraid I might see his body. No sign of Kean, but the inside of his apartment was a mess. In that moment, Holly dropped my hand and ran ahead to our door. With one quick push, our door opened wide. Chaos! The television and stereo, my wedding rings, jewelry, and leather jackets: all gone, along with numerous, small items, long since forgotten. It was my mother's birthday, November 14. I had been planning to call her that night. Two months later to the date, after friends and family had helped to replace our TV, stereo, and a couple of pieces of jewelry as Christmas presents, I was shocked to come home and once again find it all gone. Relieved of my lease obligation for obvious reasons, Holly and I moved out.

It was a memorable search for a new apartment as a single woman with one child. Call after call produced the same conversation:

"How many people are you?"

"There are two of us: myself and my two-year-old daughter."

"What? No husband? Oh no!"

"But I have a job, I can pay the rent."

Click.

And we thought San Francisco was so progressive! Persistent, we moved into a great apartment on Warren Drive with a garage, on-property laundry facilities, and a wooded hillside behind us. I never closed the curtains and soaked in the weather, seasonal flowers, and wildlife on that hillside for over six years, and we were never ripped off the entire time. I allowed that sense of security to soothe me and I felt at home for the first time in a long while.

She Had "Love" Tattooed on Her Body

Eighty-five-year-old Julia was a stately woman. Purse hanging from her forearm, she walked the halls on the tenth-floor oncology unit of St. Francis Memorial Hospital. Cancer-ridden, like all the other patients, she held her head high. Certain she was at the St. Francis hotel, but not quite remembering the way to the lobby, she would stop by my desk at the nurse's station to ask for directions. Julia was undoubtedly remembering her more beautiful life. I believe it must have been quite elegant.

Some of the caregivers—too busy to be entertained by Julia's antics and eccentricities—could be thoughtless and dismissive in their dealings with her. Their lack of patience, kindness, or reverence for this once elegant woman disturbed me. At twenty-eight, I thought of Julia with a respect I didn't fully understand, but in her honor and with my own future in mind, I had a small, spontaneously selected tiger lily tattooed on my right breast.

My tattoo wasn't the most perfect, but it was done by Lyle Tuttle, the infamous artist himself. His days of San Francisco glory were waning and his talent was now questionable, but off I went after work with my girlfriends Lu and Marilyn to his studio at Seventh and Market Street, stone-cold sober. (Should have known better, but I didn't drink much then.)

My thinking went a little like this: *When I am old and wandering the hospital halls in search of my former, beautiful life, I want the people caring for me to know that I once had some spunk and a vibrant life of love and adventure.* I thought the originality of a tattoo on a woman would convey that. Little did I know that years later, nearly every girl on the planet would be tattooed from head to toe, and I would just seem unimaginative with my one imperfect tiger lily that became a rose when I tried to perfect it.

A few months after getting settled in our new home, I got offered a position as the medical transcriber in the radiation oncology department and was happy to leave the tenth floor. I was neither a transcriptionist nor much of a typist, but on a closed floor in a former hospital room now wedged into a pseudo office, I sat alone and learned. Periodically, the chief of security would stop by to check on me. That job continued to expand my interest in caring for cancer patients and launched what became my career in health care billing and administration.

When the closed hospital floor reopened with patient beds, my office was moved across the street into an old apartment building the hospital had purchased. It was a studio with a full kitchen and bath and room for two large desks with a window facing the street and the front door of the hospital. While typing and on the phone, I saw everything and everyone coming and going. Sometimes I watched the door in anticipation. Sometimes who I saw approaching brought a smile to my face and a jazzy beat to my heart.

Clarissa Pinkola Estés, author of *Women Who Run with the Wolves*, reminds us that our experiences in life are like doors—doors we can open into our deeper selves, our wild selves. We can explore old stories about ourselves, what fills us with passion and, I believe, even what scares us. By being bold and writing my way through fear and through my own, deep-rooted narratives, the doors that have opened in my life remind me of my resilience and my desire to choose love.

ACT IV

Love Prevails

When Holly was about three and a half, I began dating GB Ayers. He was the chief administrative technologist and the head of the radiology department at St. Francis. You could say we were neighbors: I worked for the department of radiation oncology next door. I already knew him casually enough to say hello and, in passing, bask in the warmth of his smile.

GB was held in high regard all over the hospital. Tall and handsome in his lab coat and tie, he walked with an easy smile and friendly offers of assistance to his staff, colleagues, patients, and friends. As he strode through the halls on his way to management meetings and problem-solving sessions, I always said his generous spirit made every woman feel like "queen for a day." No matter how busy he was, he was kind and took his time with people.

GB had recently separated from his wife of sixteen years. After a few dates, he told me they were still trying to work things out. He would understand if I didn't want to keep seeing him. I told him that I would never fight his wife for him. If he could resolve a sixteen-year relationship, I wouldn't blame him for trying again. We continued to see each other, however, and eventually, his wife became his ex. A few months later, GB would leave the temporary apartment he had been renting since his separation and move in with Holly and me.

Before he moved in, I gave my mom an update over the phone. "GB and I have decided to live together. He'll be moving in next week."

"Are you sure you want to do that again?" she asked.

I paused, understanding that GB had two strikes against him in her estimation and she hadn't even met him. "He's Black and he's ten years older than you," she said. Eddie was nine years older. "Why would you want to do that again?"

"He's a good man and we love each other, Mom."

Perhaps her response had been predictable, but as usual, I never saw it coming. Could she never just be happy for me?

I could imagine her pursed lips as she changed the subject and began talking about the pot roast she had cooked on Tuesday and would be warming up for dinner that night. This diversion tactic was typical. My mother could never stay with the hard stuff long enough to gain an understanding or share some love. Even when I had called her in deep pain over Eddie dying, she would quickly move to talk about what was cooking on the stove. Her lack of emotional availability or support would remain painful and stupidly surprising throughout my life.

Despite his congeniality, GB was humble and a bit of a loner, going to kung fu movies by himself on Saturday afternoons, buying cars, and perusing used book and record stores for quintessential jazz albums and random editions. He could take things apart and fix anything. One day, while dropping Holly off at Rooftop Elementary School, he opened the driver's door on his Volvo and another parent slammed into it. He later went to the auto wrecking yard, found a blue door, strung up a pully system in the garage of our apartment building, and installed that junkyard door by himself. He drove the white car with the faded navy blue door until he sold it a few years later, having gone out one afternoon and buying us a previously owned Mercedes.

The blue door was one of many little projects GB left unfinished. His house projects often remained not-quite-complete as well. Like how long after painting a room before the doorknobs go back on? Or why did one wall in the den never get spackled after we stripped eighty-five years of layered wallpaper off in preparation for painting? Little things got left undone that I lovingly called his "signature pieces."

Our relationship was playful. We developed traditions and house rules . . . like deciding that KFC for dinner was only acceptable if served with champagne and appliances and tools only counted as gifts on Tuesdays—never for birthdays or holidays. Compelled to love our way through this life as an interracial couple, we found a method for attending to strangers' ridiculously obvious attention: the burden for those who choose to love "differently." When GB and I drove together or walked down the street hand in hand and someone stared or looked at us askance, GB would turn to me in his good-natured way, smile, and say, "Friend of yours?" Usually, we laughed at people's ignorance. We brought out the silly in each other. He thanked me for that. I credited him as he found his comfort with me and within himself.

GB was the least judgmental person I had ever met. Rarely did he say a critical word. I tried to learn that skill from him and I think I made some progress beyond my essential nature. GB gave generously of his being and his body. For years, he had a standing appointment at the blood bank and donated quarterly without fail, and he always said yes if someone needed help or a hand to move or fix something. Over the years, countless people shared stories with me of his generosity: something GB had done or said that had made a difference in their lives, a kindness extended, or a visit he'd made when they were sick. They always assumed that I knew the story they were telling me, but these stories were new ones to me. His humility prevented him from ever boasting about all that he did for others.

During a beautiful, backyard memorial service for our friend David McAlexander, David's partner singled out GB for being especially supportive during David's final days. David had been on the management team of the hospital and represented one of our early, devastating losses to AIDS. While GB had always brought me home David's handmade "McTruffles," I was un-aware of GB's extra visits or all the ways he'd helped David during that difficult time. In moments like that—such as listening to David's eulogy—I might have felt outside of GB's world. But I also felt proud. Happy that I was the one he came home to. I have never respected a human being more than I respected GB Ayers.

GB and I spent ten years loving each other, years that made me feel lucky. I felt supported. I felt fully myself. We made deci-sions easily and built a life of friends and family. We had a bump now and then, but no drama like I'd had in my past or his. After all, GB was largely conflict-avoidant and would sooner go for a walk than argue. I learned to let him go, and later, we would talk. My upsets had more to do with his long work hours and his un-willingness to leave the office at the end of a long day, sentiments that changed once I started doing similar work with the same level of dedication. When issues became a bigger deal, we worked those ones out too: whatever it was, we handled it together.

GB is the only father Holly remembers. She let him into her childhood heart. He became her ally, often calming my fears and encouraging me to let her try things, helping to loosen my over-protective tendencies. He also managed his frustrations when she would act out or try to put distance between them. The three of us became a family and we were surrounded by caring friends.

GB was my perfect match—with one exception. He didn't think he wanted to have a child and I did. Children had not been in his life plan, despite the fact that he had helped raise his ex-wife's daughter and nurtured and secured Holly's love and trust. What's more, all my girlfriend's kids were crazy about him. But after we'd been together for almost four years, my biological clock was ticking, so much so I was pressuring myself about whether or not to stay with GB or break up and hope to meet someone else who wanted to have children with me. These concerns preyed on my mind.

On Friday, November 13, 1981, GB and I made love early in the morning and I left on a road trip with two girlfriends. Kathy was moving to Seattle and Marilyn and I were going to help her and then go to visit my parents in Bellingham for a few days. While I was on that trip, I came to terms with myself and my desire to have another child, and I let it go. GB was too important to my life. I loved him and being with him was what I wanted most. We already had Holly, and in another ten years, she would be off to college and we could continue enjoying life, traveling, and growing old together. Rationale complete, my issue resolved: I could be happy without another child. GB was my rock, my joy, my partner, and the reflection of my best self.

A couple of weeks later, I woke up at 3:00 a.m., that magic hour of communing with the angels. I got up and sat quietly on the living room couch and knew that I was pregnant. It was an intuitive knowing, because my period was about five minutes late. We were on our way out the door to one of our many Christmas parties when I got the call from the lab confirming that hunch. Until then, GB had been holding his breath, saying, "Well, we really don't know." I knew. Soon we would have our most

difficult conversations yet. Would we have a baby? Without resolution or anger, we moved quietly into our distinct uncertainties.
One weekend, I drove to Monterey to visit my grandmother and
take some time for myself. On the drive, I connected with the
soul that I understood would be our son.

When I got home, I told GB that I was going to have the baby.
I told him that he was free to decide if he wanted to participate, but
either way, I was going ahead. He was quiet for a few more days—
long, uncertain days for me, quiet and personal days for him as we
each awaited his decision. I was unwavering in my choice. But when
he said, "Yes . . . I'll do my best," I was ecstatic. We would be growing our family together. GB took a little longer to get his sense of
humor back, but all along, I cajoled him. "It's okay, honey," I
teased. "We've got this. Just say 'baay-beee.' Baby!"

And from there, we rolled with it: right into Lamaze classes
and plans for a "natural childbirth" in a San Francisco alternative
birth center. Auntie Marilyn, my sister-girlfriend since our early
days working at Children's Hospital, would be seven-and-a-half-
year-old Holly's birth partner and Claudia, the head nurse who'd
hired me at St. Francis and a member of my women's group,
would be our "event" photographer. Suellen, a friend from grad
school, was a midwife. We were all set. I pushed through those
next two semesters and six weeks before our son was born, graduated a semester early with my master's degree. GB's colleagues
and our friends from the hospital threw a surprise baby shower
and our friend Judy hosted another. Everyone was celebrating our
baby and so were we. I like to think God knew what was best for
us and what I would need going forward. Our son has been a
major life blessing.

Love Grows

Bryan sparked love at first sight. His birth had been an astounding event, and even went more or less as planned—as much as birthing a nine-pound, six-ounce baby could. This included Claudia experiencing camera malfunctions while trying to take birthing photos, so she'd shifted her role to offer physical support. Unfortunately, she reeked of clove cigarettes and became an unexpected source of nausea. I had to ask her to step away. GB kept one eye on our midwife, Suellen, looking for cues that all was well and rubbing my back as we walked around the room to keep the labor moving. Holly was watchful and attentive as she applied cool towels to my forehead and offered me sips of water through a straw. Her worried little face and dark eyes never left me throughout.

The birth process turned out to be frightening for Holly. In retrospect, I might have chosen not to include her, but in the '80s, siblings were often included in family alternative births or home births. Once Bryan was born and Holly held him and was sure I wasn't dying, she grew tired and went home for a bath and a nap at Auntie Marilyn's. Beth and Grace, my women's group sisters, were among the next to arrive after getting the call from Claudia. More friends arrived and the champagne started flowing.

GB became an even more amazing father and partner. Every day after work, as soon as he got home, he would pick up baby Bryan. Then GB would cart him along to our room to keep him company while he changed out of his work clothes. He'd throw in a load of laundry, change diapers, bring home dinner: he was all in from his first yes. Bryan attended his first concert at two weeks old, a double bill with the Temptations and the Four Tops. My mother had come to visit and we had planned for her to babysit for the first time. But Bryan wasn't interested in the bottle and I didn't have the pumping process worked out yet, so off we went to introduce Bryan to Motown live. We settled into our seats for a beautiful, outdoor evening of soul under the stars. Adorable and bundled up, Bryan woke up between naps and looked around with his bright eyes. Life was sweet, our hearts were full, and our partnership was easy and loving.

We celebrated Bryan's first birthday a month after moving into our new house in Oakland. We didn't do an exhaustive search for houses and we hadn't saved much money. The house we bought had been built in 1906. A shifty real estate agent put a positive spin on the neighborhood in which it was purchased, saying that a lot of people were moving over from San Francisco and fixing up old Victorians in Oakland. "But of course," she told us, "financially, things could go either way." Things didn't go our way during that leap into the real estate market. Five years later, after painting and landscaping the outside and fully refinishing the interior—with the exception of the kitchen and bathrooms—I would sell that house for the same price we had paid: a setback most San Francisco buyers would have found outrageous at the time.

When Bryan was about two, I started working in education and training at Kaiser hospital and a year later as a practice administrator in a small start-up ophthalmology practice in San Francisco. We were enjoying our family life and each other. GB and I were good partners, we had a home with endless projects, we loved to entertain and play music, we had good jobs, friends and family, and we knew how to have fun and work through shit whenever it came up. I thought I was living my happy ending. The life I had dreamed into being, having paid my dues.

Love Expands

GB

He always kissed me when he got home, whether from work, a
run to the grocery store, or a Saturday afternoon kung fu
movie on his own.
A gentle kiss usually, with his arm around my shoulder or waist,
his hands familiar and kind.
A kiss that said simply, "I'm happy to see you again."
In our bedroom, he would hang his suit and tie and change into
jeans and a T-shirt, usually one with a colorful message
(HNIC or WHERE THE HELL'S OAKLAND? for example) or
the logo from some restaurant or town we had visited and
liked. (Buster Holmes in New Orleans comes to mind.)
As we made dinner and he poured the wine, we talked of the
day.
While prepping the food, we'd brush casually against each other,
maybe with just an arm that reached for the sink or a vegeta-
ble to chop, initiating a smile, or maybe a full-belly, head-
back laugh.
With Bob James, Ahmad Jamal, or Miles Davis playing, we'd
dance and dip in the dining room.
With him, I was my best self, and it was easy being me.
He always kissed me good night.

Once upon a Time . . .

GB and I were planning a Mediterranean cruise with friends. Two weeks before we were scheduled to leave, he wasn't feeling great. Actually, for weeks or maybe longer, he hadn't looked well, often pale, his soft, sleepy brown eyes lacking luster. But he kept telling me he was okay and refusing my suggestion that he see a doctor. I discovered just how not okay he was the day he failed to fully clean away the bright red blood in the toilet bowl. A few days later, he had a colonoscopy and was diagnosed with fourth-stage colon cancer.

The day the cruise ship sailed, GB had surgery to remove the cancer, leaving him with a permanent colostomy and a treatment plan to include radiation therapy followed by chemo.

I was shattered. He was reassuring. That night in the hospital, he told me to look in his closet on the top shelf when I got home. There, he had hidden my birthday present. A pair of small diamond earrings and Anita Baker's "Giving You the Best That I Got" cassette tape. Not the happy birthday he had planned for our cruise. Over the next year, I played the tape on repeat as I drove to and from the hospital at all hours. I cried my heart out every time.

My anguish was familiar territory. I knew well enough to appreciate our time together as cancer once again threatened to steal a life I cherished. GB and I packed a lot of love into the next fifteen months.

Still, it was a struggle for me to stay positive. I tried—for GB and for the kids. He stayed strong and diligently worked between therapies, and since his radiation and chemo usually took place in the hospital where he worked, he needed only to go down the hall, have his treatment, and return to his desk. Until cancer arrived, he had never called in sick to work or missed a day of school in his life. That was how he was. I think his dedication kept him going and kept him alive—beyond the doctors' expectations.

Birthdays and holidays came and went, even when all I could think about was each celebration possibly being the last. Friends were immediately and continuously supportive. They took Bryan on playdates and Holly on girlfriend overnights, just letting them have some time away from home and giving GB and me time alone. They also gave me time to hope, pray, and meditate on his healing. Or have a glass of wine and try to figure it all out—all the while wondering how this could be my life. GB and I found reasons to laugh, seeking a lightness that often eluded us, and over time, outside of caring for and spending time with my husband and kids, my usual pursuits fell into obscurity. My world became smaller than ever as we focused on cancer and our time together and the next metaphorical mountain to climb.

GB and I didn't share any particular faith or religion, but as the years passed, we were sorting out our spiritual beliefs together. We'd been creating our own traditions. Most Sundays as we were getting the day started, GB would say, "You ready for your Sunday-morning uplift?" With that, he'd put Aretha Franklin's *Amazing Grace* album on the turntable, followed by Sunday jazz or other gospel records from our collection. GB and I played music of all different genres in our home, creating a running soundtrack of the life we were sharing with our children.

At home in our usual peace after the kids were in bed, we'd light candles, and with headsets on, we'd lie together on the couch, massaging each other's feet and listening to guided, healing meditations. At least, I was meditating. Turns out GB was often listening to Aretha or jazz. We cracked up when I busted him, pulling back his headphones to whisper in his ear and catching the rich sound of Ella Fitzgerald's scatting.

You could say music was our religion, and for me, Stevie Wonder came as close to God as I had been so far. We had seen Stevie several times in person. Once at the Circle Star Theater, an intimate, rotating theater-in-the-round, Stevie invited any kids in the audience to join him on stage. That night we had taken Holly with us to the concert, and with a little encouragement, she shyly entered the spotlight. She stood next to the inimitable Stevie Wonder at the piano and sang "Ebony and Ivory." Holly knew every word, and what's more, she could sing—her moment a jubilant one for her and her parents, and for Stevie too, I like to think. In terms of spiritual awareness, GB and I shared a belief in the purposeful nature of life and the generosity of being kind and helpful to others. But most of all, we believed that music would take you where nothing else would. Music was both a means and an end: we weren't worried about heaven or hell.

While GB was going through treatment, we attended a three-day *Healing into Life and Death* workshop with Stephen Levine, my spiritual leader eleven years earlier, and his wife, Ondrea. The workshop focused on mindfulness meditation, pain and grief, and healing the heart and mind through awareness and acceptance. I was looking for the strength to endure, or at least a measure of peace and understanding. I found temporary tranquility until we pulled into the driveway at home and Holly ran out yelling, "Grandma and Grandpa are on the phone!"

Now anyone who has attended healing workshops knows that after days in such deep and altering states, one should be mindful of one's fragility. But as soon as I heard Holly's words, I foolishly ran in to take their call. Since 1974, I had avoided all discussions with my parents regarding their support of the Vietnam War and

Richard Nixon. Oddly enough, while driving home from the workshop that day, it had occurred to me that if my stepfather could just forgive Jane Fonda for her activism during the Vietnam War, he would have so much more energy to love. (Ha! Let me change the world!) On that call, politics became the focus once I'd mentioned Jane Fonda's name, and I had one of the most vicious fights with my parents to date. All the while, my niece, Kami, who had been with Holly and Bryan while we were away, kissed me goodbye on my tear-wet cheek and GB put the kids to bed and filled my wineglass. Note to self: beware of your own good intentions after devotional time in the mountains on a meditation cushion.

After nine years together, and three months since GB's cancer diagnosis, we decided to get married. Quietly, we thought. Just stop at city hall in Oakland on the way to the hospital for yet another admission. We were somehow foiled by the process that day, so we headed across the Bay Bridge to the hospital in San Francisco with only the Alameda County license in hand and no marriage certificate. A disappointment in the scheme of things, but we were short on time and couldn't be late for GB's doctor appointment and admission to the hospital.

I happened to work across the street from the hospital where GB was admitted. After getting Holly and Bryan to their destinations each morning, I would drive to San Francisco and see GB before going to my office, returning for lunch and every evening at the end of my day. On January 6, 1987, a couple of scary days after GB's most recent admission, I went to my office and was fired.

I had been talking with the doctor I worked for all along, concerned that he needed more than I was able to offer while GB
was sick. Time and again, my employer had reassured me that my
job was secure and not to worry. But he had lied and hired my
replacement. I had seen him early one morning at a café on Fillmore Street having coffee with a manager from an office upstairs.
My intuition was right, as usual. So was my understanding of what
he needed. He just couldn't admit his intentions to me until he
had someone else lined up. Packing my things in a box—knowing
my employer had only released me from obligations I hadn't been
able to walk away from myself—I told him, "I know I will thank
you one of these days. But right now, I think you're a real ass." A
few years later, my former boss told a doctor I was interviewing
with that he had fired me because I was unavailable when my
husband had cancer. *Still an ass!* The docs I was interviewing with
thought so too. I got that job, and they rather comically told me
about his comments later. I would be their practice administrator
for the next seven years.

Back at the hospital with GB sooner than expected that morning, I was there when the chaplain dropped in as chaplains do. We
told him about our failed plan to get married a few days earlier.
"I'll do it!" he said. "You just have to get the San Francisco license." He offered to marry us that afternoon.

Cynthia had been a sister-girlfriend of my heart for years, always a loving part of our family, a big GB fan, and the first person
I called three months earlier when we learned the diagnosis. That
day, she left her job at lunch, picked me up at the hospital, and
whisked me off to city hall to obtain a marriage license. Our friend
Tom Payne, on his way to have a root canal, stopped by the hospital to visit GB. Realizing a surprise was in the works, he bailed
on his dental appointment and went shopping for champagne,

glasses, and a cake. The nurses were buzzing amid the unusual festivities, pulling crepe paper decorations from drawers and running to the cafeteria for plates and forks. The minister arrived with a beautiful bouquet of white roses for me. The groom wore gray flannel pajamas with a matching robe and IV pole. The bride, fashionable in the ivory silk blouse and purple wool pencil skirt she had worn to work that morning. Fired and married all in the same unpredictable day.

I didn't know our relationship could be better, but somehow getting married took it to a new level, a deeper love we didn't anticipate. If we had, we might have done it sooner. Until then, getting married had not been our priority. Following my previous husband's death, the law indicated that if I didn't remarry, I would remain eligible for spousal social security—a boon while I was in school getting my master's degree and working an unpaid internship at a women's center, then again when Bryan was born and before I was ready to go back to work. Now, through the lens of planning for a grim future, getting married offered protection for our son, daughter, and me. I was surprised to learn that a piece of paper would come to mean so much more for us than just common sense.

GB and I were married for one year and twenty days of our ten years together. Our focus was on life, our family, and each other, until it was torn apart by the fear of his death and the pain of cancer and its treatment. In August 1987, we celebrated Bryan's fifth birthday with a big party in the park at our neighborhood recreation center. Music, presents, food, piñatas, ice cream, and a Spider-Man cake: family and friends—just like normal. A friend videotaped all the fun, knowing it would likely be Bryan's last birthday with his dad. In September, we celebrated GB's fiftieth birthday with a party and the usual crowd of friends. In October,

GB hosted my thirty-ninth birthday with a joint surprise party for Cynthia and me at our home, complete with dinner, corsages, champagne, and cake. In November, we celebrated Holly's thirteenth birthday with her usual slumber party and a houseful of girls. Like every other year we had been together, busy holidays followed our sequential birthday months, busy even though we knew time was short.

Throughout GB's illness, friends were by our sides, showing up with food and wine. Lots of wine was required throughout this ordeal. Just ask Sonja who showed up with an endless supply of Viognier, pâté, and cornichons. Calls, cards, and letters came daily from GB's many fans at the hospital, as did flowers, fruit, and cheese baskets.

We were well loved and full of gratitude. We had a wonderful team of caring doctors, many who were big fans and friends of ours from work, and we had a kind hospice team once further treatment was no longer a consideration. But we were dying. GB of colon cancer and me of a broken heart.

Grief

Grief lives alongside a calendar that once tracked fun with
    friends, visits, adventures, and vacations.
It slips in between commitments and promises, plans and ideas,
    sandwiched by shoulds and must-dos.
Grief ends up in the suitcase, pulls up a chair at the dinner table,
    arrives in the mail and drains away thoughts and energy.
Grief uproots faith and challenges the best intentions of the day.
Grief watches children become adults.

Grief smiles through tears, languishes on beaches, and rattles the
ice at the bottom of my drink.

Grief suns itself lazily alongside my body.

Grief sets the table and dances alone in the kitchen.

Grief remembers the name of my beloved, his laughter and love,
counsel and companionship.

Grief ambushes the moment when I sense my breath, call for
the strength of my spirit, or feel the heat and heartbeat of my
body.

Grief rambles gently, then withers in moments when joy expands for no good reason.

Love Says Goodbye

GB died at home on January 26, 1988, his mother from Detroit
asleep upstairs in our bedroom, my parents from Bellingham on
the sofa bed in our living room, the kids in their rooms, my
brother Robert on the floor in the dining room, and GB and I in
our den, where we had been on the sofa bed for months once
he'd grown unable to go up the stairs.

The last days can be tricky when you're exhausted and know
the time is coming. GB battled his demons and fear after a year
of denial and putting up such a brave front and strong fight. The
waning of the fight took a couple of days but felt like a lifetime.
He stared at me, his face emaciated and terror searing out of his
soft brown eyes. I witnessed him trying to come to terms with his
death and held him, containing my own fright and panic and the
deep sadness that lived in every cell of my body. Once he had
passed through that portal of acceptance, he grew peaceful. I

understand the anguish that precedes surrender is often part of the dying process.

Family and friends had been saying their last goodbyes for days. Holly was aware that he would die soon, and she did not want to be gone when that happened. She was scheduled to spend the weekend at Auntie Marilyn's with her girlfriend Tiffany and was worried about leaving. GB assured her. "Not this weekend, maybe Monday or Tuesday," he said. "You go have fun at Auntie Marilyn's. I'll be here when you get home." He kept his promise as usual.

Monday night, Robert and I sat near GB talking in hushed voices until about 3:00 a.m. Worn and bleary-eyed, Robert went to his sleeping bag in the dining room. I lay down in bed beside GB with my arm linked through his at the elbow. I closed my eyes. I believe I traveled with GB out of his body, out of mine, and beyond time. I don't know how long I was out there in the great beyond with him, but from far, far away, I heard Holly and Bryan fussing at the bathroom door, trying to negotiate who got to go in first. It was a Tuesday, just before 7:00 a.m. on a school day. With a clunk, I fell partway back into my body and hurried across the room to shush them before fully grounding back to Earth. Argument settled, I came back to our bed. A trace of one dried tear trailed down GB's cool cheek. He was gone. Tears flowing, I rested on his shoulder and held my husband before tiptoeing around and waking the others and telling my children that their father had died.

Later that morning, GB's mother called a friend to pick her up. The next time I saw her she was at the memorial with his sisters and brother who had just flown in to join her. I got busy "making arrangements" and would stay busy for the rest of my life.

Family Love Tested

GB's family hadn't exactly been close, but his death was hard on them. After graduating from high school, he'd left Detroit to enlist in the air force. In the thirty-odd intervening years, GB had changed. He'd told me that he couldn't find work once he'd returned home, so he came out to Oakland, California, to see a woman he'd met while stationed in Arizona—a woman who would become his wife. In the years before GB and I met, I think he'd made two trips back to Detroit, once for his father's funeral, and maybe one other time; I don't remember the reason. But in the ten years we spent together, he didn't go back to see his family once. My suggestions that we visit were always met with a laugh and a joke about Detroit being "too hot . . . summer might come early or too cold . . . might be a long winter." But the final answer was always "No—not interested." We invited his family to visit us and each of his sisters came out. They stayed in our home, and we had fun showing them all the sights in San Francisco and the Bay Area. Now and then, I encouraged him to call his family and he would.

When Bryan was born, GB's sisters and mother came out to visit. They celebrated our new baby and I believed they felt welcome and loved in our home. Grandma Daisy made a hand-stitched baby quilt, with rabbits embroidered in thick white thread, and everything seemed family-like in a good way.

Four years later, when GB was diagnosed with colon cancer, each of his three siblings came to California, once to see him, then again for his memorial. Often, our exchanges felt strained. His family apparently couldn't accept the man GB had become and seemed to blame me for his lack of religious affiliation. Like many families, theirs did not communicate freely and steered away from questions that might lead to discovery or even disagreement, including questions about religion. I had no idea that religion would be the problem. I have seen how families are often fixed in how they know one another, and struggle when forced to face change and differences.

Even when you live authentically and have nothing to hide, people can choose to remain blind to what they don't want to see—such as the presence of love. And what they do see can quickly be misinterpreted. Take the Ouija board Cynthia had given Holly for her birthday that year. One glimpse at this board and I was deemed a witch and the reason GB would not make it into heaven. His sisters then sent him a beautiful, leather-bound, engraved Bible and gave our phone number to local and distant COGIC (Church of God in Christ) ministers, who began calling to come to pray so that GB could accept Jesus Christ as his savior and get through the gates of heaven. Those requests were met with a polite "No thank you." It wasn't our way. His goodness in life had surely paved his way to whatever goodness awaited him on the other side.

An open-casket funeral had not been his choice, either. Over the last few days of his life, I asked GB to talk with his family about his wish to be cremated. His response was classic GB: "Oh, they'll be all right."

"No, they won't, and they aren't!" I pushed back. As it turned out, his family was never "all right" with me again.

I hoped that the love of about two hundred people who arrived for GB's memorial service would penetrate his family's hurt and release their fears of his lost soul in the afterlife. When our friend Bill Stewart stood at the podium and said to the crowd, "I don't know where you all came from; I thought *I* was his best friend!" and everyone laughed and knew what Bill meant, I hoped his mother, sisters, and brother would have a sense of the man that GB was. I hoped they could see the evidence of his thoughtfulness and consideration of others. I hoped that the many friends, family, and colleagues who spoke of his grace, his acts of kindness, and the many ways my husband had touched their lives would console his family. I hoped that his family would be lifted up by the voice of my niece singing "Amazing Grace" and "Love Lift Us Up," and by our son's call out when she finished—"That was great, Kami!"—as the room burst into the sweet relief that only five-year-old Bryan could inspire. But these were only my hopes and they went unrewarded.

The day after GB's memorial, his family stopped by on their way to the airport. They exchanged cordial greetings with the friends and family who were hanging out the way people do when someone has died and no one knows what to do except hang around, eat and drink, take out the garbage, wash dishes, do laundry, and find some practical way to be helpful and comforting. His mother, brother, and sisters took seats at the dining room table and sat quietly talking, mostly among themselves about me.

Danny came upstairs to let me know that they had arrived. "They don't like white people," my Black brother-in-law explained. I don't know if his words were true, and I had not felt their sting in the past, but they all behaved awkwardly with me, and my Black and white friends and family knew it. They whispered, but as a sister picked up a photo of Bryan, I overheard her say, "GB never wanted kids. How did she talk him into that?" They all agreed that I was a bad influence: because of me, he had changed from his upbringing and their religious beliefs; "He should have been in church." Crushed and infuriated, I remained silent and said polite goodbyes, guessing I would not be hearing from my in-laws anytime soon. I may have thought that would be just fine with me, but when Holly called GB's brother a month or two later—a man she had called Uncle—and he didn't return her call, it wasn't fine with me at all. My in-laws' dismissal felt cruel.

We never heard from GB's family again. It would be nearly twenty years before my son would reach out and make the healing journey to meet with his father's family in Detroit. Bryan opened that door on his own and walked through it with all the grace and sense of self that he needed to set things right. He built relationships and connected with them. I'm happy for him and I think they were happy to meet the man he has become. So fully himself yet such a strong reminder of his dad.

Over the years, I have explored and observed many ways that people find God and seek comfort in life and death. In much of North America, few traditions either prepare us for death or support us in the experience. Life skills and values are unique and individually developed as well. With that understanding, I have forgiven GB's family but maintain that anything that causes separation, including religion, is in denial of our true nature, which is to love one another.

Absent Love

When GB died, I weighed 104 pounds and bought a size-four black print dress to wear to his memorial. I was just over five-foot-seven and usually up to thirty-five pounds heavier. After being concerned about my weight for most of my life, I watched with some fascination as my body evaporated. Despite exhaustion and heartbreak, survival required me to stay busy. I focused first on finishing all the overdue house projects and landscaping so I wouldn't be reminded that I would now be facing them alone. Landscapers and contractors working at my home attracted the attention of the neighborhood bad guys, who now included our next-door neighbor. Our house had been burglarized twice when we'd first moved in, and since I had no man around now, they were continually assessing the situation.

I braved my way through the completion of house projects with the support of alert and protective contractors, and on GB's birthday, nearly eight months after his death, I held a party to celebrate. My tender new lawn took a bit of a beating that afternoon, but it was nice to have the house and yard full of friends in celebration of GB and the beauty of my house and garden project.

Finishing the projects, however, did not make me any more comfortable or less afraid. Turns out the next-door neighbor had been regularly asking GB for money. When he approached me, I wasn't as forthcoming and I hoped he would understand. I came home one day just after he had thrown a rock through my living room window preparing to climb in, claiming he had chased away the guy who had done it. On several occasions, people had pounded alarmingly on my front door in the middle of the night calling out for help. From my upstairs bedroom window, I offered to call the police, and strangers walked casually off my porch using threatening gestures and language to let me know what they thought of that suggestion.

I felt too vulnerable and fresh out of the fierceness it took for me to live in that house without GB. I started looking for a new home. The day the For Sale sign went up and I opened the detached garage at the end of the driveway to get a shovel for the real estate agent, three men came out and walked past me and down the driveway, pointing at the house next door, saying they were "just going over to Daryl's," like that should explain every-thing. They had broken through the fence and the back wall of the garage and were apparently living in there and using it as a shortcut to the house next door. Crack is an insidious drug.

Adding to my fear was thirteen-year-old Holly's behavior. She had lost two fathers in her short lifetime. Having lost my father at her age, and later, two husbands, I tried to understand. GB was the only father Holly remembered and to the extent she was able, she gave him that place in her life. She also kept him as a kind of "placeholder" for her "real dad" and always called GB by his name. Holly told me that she had always wanted to call GB Dad, but was unsure and confused by a misperceived need to remain loyal to Eddie's family, who were still a significant part of our lives. She was also trying to create a degree of detachment, scared of death and thinking that if "something bad happened to GB and we're not that close, I'll be okay."

Holly was grieving, and I wanted to love her through her pain, but she didn't seem to want me anywhere near her. She was angry, and like me, she couldn't understand why—once again—someone she loved had died. As she was able to articulate it years later, she had lost her ally and the person she trusted to help her navigate the world and her relationship with me. "With GB in our life, we made sense," she told me. A Black dad, a white mom, and two mixed-race children of different hues and heads of hair. How we had looked as a family made sense—our genetic connection was obvious—and without GB, we didn't. Now she hated being asked "what she was mixed with."

Until middle school, our family and many of her friends' fam-ilies were interracial and from multicultural families. All races were harmonious and together and all seemed normal—as it should be. That perspective changed for Holly when she started in a predominantly white middle school where, for the first time, she was made to feel "different."

As a freshman in high school, Holly began lying about using alcohol and smoking cigarettes, and I wasn't sure what else. She blamed the neighbor girl's mother for the acrid smells she was wearing home. When I would accuse her, she was ready to fight and her eyes would turn dark and away.

Some of Holly's behavior had started while GB was sick; the worst of her acting out usually occurred when my parents were visiting. Twice, they'd come to stay with Holly and Bryan so I could remain at the hospital with GB for a surgery or treatment, but on both trips, things didn't go well. When I would call home, my mom was usually upset with Holly, saying, "Holly ran off to a neighbor's house and refuses to come home for dinner." "Holly won't listen to me or Grandpa." "Holly didn't do what I told her to." *Holly this and Holly that!* I wanted Holly to be part of what was happening, not another problem to deal with. Confused and upset, I couldn't understand why she was adding to the already-difficult situation. Why wouldn't she let her grandparents comfort her or help us? After all, that's why the grandparents were there.

She began getting into more trouble at school in her freshman year; her grades were going down and the teachers were continually calling me with reports of her incomplete work and difficult attitude. Holly was smart and had always done well in school, testing in the advanced levels and taking AP classes. She loved sports, theater, dance, and gymnastics and had been in classes, on teams, and performing since she was a little girl. She also had a wild streak. By age three, she could be a handful: planting herself firmly on the floor of Macy's and refusing to move, screaming and kicking when I picked her up until she slithered out of my arms and back onto the floor. Or, while Auntie Marilyn drove us across the

Bay Bridge, putting her hand on my mouth and screaming repeatedly when I removed it or tried to hold it, "I want my hand on your mouth!" (Those were the days before car seats, when children commonly rode in cars by sitting on their parent's lap.) I took her to therapy, but in 1977, they had few insights or strategies to offer young children or their parents. After a few sand play sessions, I was assured that her three-year-old temper tantrums and strong will were normal. As she got older and continued pushing the limits with me, in my desperation, we tried therapy again and again in various family formations that included GB and sometimes Bryan. Holly hated therapy and our efforts usually ended up with just me working on me.

Now Holly was struggling and making poor decisions for herself, and she seemed to have no regard for how difficult she was making life for me. I wanted us to grieve together and to love our way through this loss. She seemed so angry, and I was depleted and heartbroken. Again, I found myself a therapist. No therapy prepared me for what we were really dealing with and what I would soon learn.

Love Aches

The after-death ceremonies ended and the family members went home. Some not to be heard from again. It seemed I was to get on with my life. Somehow. Pull myself up by my bootstraps. What a stupid idea. Who has bootstraps? And yet everyone knows what this expression means—I guess. I knew what it meant. Time to get on with my life. Do what I have to do, what I'm supposed to do. And what exactly am I supposed to do after my love is gone?

1. Seek God.
2. Reject God.
3. Find a church—cry uncomfortably in public.
4. Reject church—too much hugging of strangers.
5. Get the kids to school.
6. Get a job.
7. Meditate.
8. Talk to a therapist.
9. Go to the grocery store.
10. Go to a friend's.
11. Feed our sick dog, Whitney—the one who peed in GB's Volvo on the way home from the shelter.
12. Put the sick dog down. Feel guilty forever for having nothing left to give her.
13. Do the laundry.
14. Cry.
15. Smile.
16. Fake it 'til you make it.
17. Acknowledge your grief.
18. Remember that everything is temporary.
19. Read another book—escape or find the answer, any answer.
20. Take life one day at a time.

I'm angry, but I must hide that part. No one wants to hear it anymore. I'm living a life I didn't want or expect. How do I love the life I have? Always the mystery. I have my kids. That's the part I come back to—that's the part that keeps me going. We get dressed. I take them to school. I look for signs to convince myself that they're doing okay. I'm so lost in the okayness of everything. What is okay about a life that ended with the death of my husband? Not one damn thing. But my life isn't over, and the lives of my children are just getting started. This is my new reality.

I do what I'm supposed to do. I pull myself together, stand up straight, put on a suit and a smile, and I get a job. I do the one thing I can do, independent of my heartache. I go to work where I have just enough confidence left. I organize, set goals, provide instruction and leadership, and I respond appropriately to my boss. I want to do a good job; I care and try to believe that what I do matters. I show up. I'm good at showing up. I smile and get pretty good at that too. I'm good at finding solutions to short-term problems, making money for other people, advocating, and making various initiatives appear to be heading in the right direction. But how the hell do I know? I do not love my life. But I do what I can and put one foot in front of the other and that seems to be enough.

A particular and unexpected vulnerability arises in telling people that before you were forty, you've had two husbands die of cancer. Oddly, the first impulse many demonstrate is to laugh—or to stifle a laugh, to let a laugh hover around their face until they regain their composure. They are embarrassed by their response to my loss. They are embarrassed by my loss. They change the subject or grasp at something more appropriate. They become even more uncomfortable. They look away. Suddenly, my job is to make them feel okay with their discomfort, the awkwardness of the moment. The other impulse is a syrupy attempt at sincerity, an effort to convey compassion and recover from their embarrassment, but it's the effort it took that gives them away.

It's the best they can do in the moment. I understand and I try to relieve them of their struggle.

I thought women would be more compassionate in the moment of telling, but that isn't always the case. Women are just as uncomfortable with grief as men are, and both have responded to my confession with variations on the following: "Was it your cooking?" Hahaha! "What did you do to those poor guys?" Hahaha! "So you're the real Black widow!" Hahaha! So obnoxious. So confusing. I quit telling. But that doesn't work, either.

I found it inconceivable—that losing my loves could be a secret too shameful to admit. My pain was one thing. The shame of my loss, a shock. How did I go from the loss of my beloved husband to becoming untouchable? Men said I was "intimidating," too "self-sufficient." They were actually encountering the shell around my heart and my show of confidence to the world.

I do not love this life. I want my life with GB back. But I can't have that. Will someone else do? I had a short-term boyfriend about a year after GB's death. I have had years of short-term boyfriends and one engagement. Lacking the depth and sense of myself I felt with GB, these relationships lit me up briefly, then ended abruptly—unceremoniously. Like candles snuffed out, one after another.

Loving Kindness

After GB died, I attended a retreat on loss and that's where I last saw Stephen Levine in person. Nourished by nature, beauty, wisdom, and amazing food at the Mount Madonna Yoga Retreat Center in the Santa Cruz Mountains, about two hundred people gathered to meditate, share their stories, listen to the wisdom of Steven and Ondrea, and heal. For the second time, I had lost my husband to cancer and was struggling with the "Why me?" blues. How could this happen to me twice?

I experienced two remarkable things at that retreat. First, people shared stories of unimaginable loss and knocked me out of my certainty that my experience was as bad as it could get. It wasn't. Stephen then opened a door to personal understanding. "Maybe GB needed someone with your level of experience to help him through," he said to me. Heavenly relief flooded my body. Stephen guided me to understand that my love for GB was both purposeful and generous. His wisdom made my grief so much more bearable. Stephen was a master guide into the open heart of awareness, mercy, and kindness, helping us all to frame loss and grief as part of life's natural cycles.

The temporary nature of everything has brought me both comfort and pain. In a world where people seek the comfort of the familiar and make major decisions based on the illusion of stability and security, holding the context that life is both personal and temporary has helped me sit with my grief and stay open to it. I began to weave a deeper understanding of what could not be undone or changed and how I could live with it. The key: loving kindness—to others and to myself.

The loving kindness meditation is an ancient Buddhist teaching intended to cultivate love and help us see our goodness and the goodness in others. It excludes no one and encompasses all life, requiring nothing in return. Loving kindness expands our awareness that all over the world, life suffers. Not only humans, but plants, insects, animals, even the Earth herself, and this awareness expands the focus of loving kindness beyond the self to all that is. The result of practicing this meditation is often the

softening of our hearts and minds. Practitioners of loving kindness meditation have experienced and documented its many other
physical, mental, and emotional benefits.

Stephen often began his meditations with the reminder to soften your belly—a tender opening for women trained all their lives
to suck their bellies in. Because participants can struggle to immediately access compassion and empathy for themselves, some
teachers, including Stephen, suggest starting the meditation by
asking students to bring to mind someone easy for them to love,
someone whose face they can see in their mind's eye and whose
love they can feel. As they sense the goodness of that person and
offer them blessings, they can more easily be filled with a loving
presence and bless themselves. When we bless ourselves, we can
move out to greater and greater expansiveness to bless all beings
and the earth.

May you be free of suffering.
May you be happy.
May you love and be loved.
May you find the healing that you seek.
May you find peace.

May I be free of suffering.
May I be happy.
May I love and be loved.
May I find the healing that I seek.
May I find peace.

May all beings everywhere be free of suffering.
May all beings be happy.
May all beings love and be loved.

May all beings find the healing that they seek.
May all beings everywhere find peace.

There are many versions of the loving kindness meditation. I find
the blessings of meditation teacher Tara Brach lovely, and I appreciate the hope and deep peace they invoke in today's troubled
times.

May I accept myself just as I am,
May I know the natural joy of being alive.
May I awaken and be free.

Loving Holly through Heartbreak

Later in the fall I began meeting with an educational consultant
to help me find a new school for Holly. Feeling defeated and angry, I planted the FOR SALE sign in our front yard and looked for
a new house. Holly, Bryan, and I moved into our new home just
before Christmas, our first holiday season after GB's death. Bryan
was now in first grade, Holly was a freshman in high school, and
I had started a new job as director of operations for a medical
device company.

In December, I visited several of the schools recommended
by the consultant who had met with Holly and had a picture of
what might be beneficial for her. I chose Cascade School, nestled
in the beautiful Cascade Mountains about forty miles east of Red-
ding, California. The school offered a well-planned two-year
therapeutic and behavioral modification program with fully ac-
credited academics. After the holiday break, Holly returned to

school at Cascade rather than Oakland Tech. She resigned herself to the idea because she knew things hadn't been going well for her, but she also thought she would only be at Cascade for six months and then home for the summer. What she didn't know then was that the program wasn't designed for short-term residential education. As we walked to the various classrooms, gathering up the signatures required to sign her out of her existing school, the teacher who had called me more often than any other smiled, waved from across the cafeteria, and said, "Nice having you, Holly. Don't work too hard!" Do you think I had any regrets about moving her to a new school? I did not.

As the view from the car window rolled by, I remember Holly saying, "Mommy, I'm a city girl. This is too country for me." She would find out just how country her new habitat was after the snow melted. Six months later, during the spring thaw, she and another girl ran away. They were lucky: picked up hitchhiking by good people who dropped the girls at the bus station, then reported their whereabouts to the police. They returned Holly and her companion safely to school.

The program at Cascade had a five-day immersive seminar format that included a specific topic at quarterly intervals. I only remember the details of one. The first seminar in the series was Truth. The students had to tell the truth to themselves, to their counselors and peers, and finally, to their parents. They had to tell the truth about what had happened to them, what they had done, why they'd lied, and whatever else they were holding and hiding that needed to be released from their bodies, their hearts, and their consciences. Shocking and devastating stories came up while sitting with the parents of the students. Hopefully, the truth coming from our children would set us all free, or at least on a less destructive path than the one that had brought us to Cascade.

I went alone on the parent weekend following their Truth intensive. Holly's job on that visit was to tell me her truth. I had been without answers for so long that I clung to the hope I'd receive the insight and understanding this weekend seemed to promise. We went for a walk on the beautiful, wooded school grounds. She told me that she had been smoking when she had said she hadn't. We kept walking. She told me that she had been drinking when she said she hadn't been. We kept walking. That was about it—except that it wasn't. After our talk, I seem to recall that we went to the pool at the Red Lion Inn with the rest of the Cascade families in town for the weekend.

A few weeks later—or maybe it was months—I got a call at work from the school saying Holly was ready to tell me her truth: the part she'd been unable to tell me in person. As her counselor handed her the phone, I looked furtively around my office. I remember the dress I had on that day. Isn't that weird? A soft gray mid-calf full skirt with long sleeves and a wide black patent-leather belt, a heavy silver multi-strand-and-stone necklace, and heels. I stood up. Then sat back down as my world fell apart.

With the support of her therapist, Holly haltingly shared the sparse and painful details of having been sexually abused from the time she was a year old. Her abusers were people I knew and loved. People, family whom I believed loved Holly. My stepfather, Ned, was included. In the hollow silence that followed—swallowed by the dark insanity of what I had just heard—I asked Holly, "Did GB ever touch you?" She responded with a startled "No, never! Mommy, why would you ask me that?" I asked her because I had to.

Holly graciously has given me permission to share her story of trauma. Out of respect for Holly's privacy, I will not infer how these events have affected her life, her experience, or her feelings.

I will share the remainder of my story as the mother of a child who was molested by people I loved and trusted—and the depth of that betrayal.

I have never been the same since that day. In that moment, my life became a lie, an illusion of the love and support I had built and relied upon. Any idea I had of myself being a "good mother" flew away. Any positive thought or regard I had for myself as a person of any value or discernment was gone. People I loved and had entrusted my children to had betrayed me and violated my beautiful daughter and I hadn't known. How on earth could that happen? How did I let that happen to her? How could I not know? Was this the price of my love?

The horror of what Holly told me that day was well beyond the grief and the sorrow I was already living with and accustomed to. Disillusionment and guilt kicked grief and sorrow to the curb, moved in, and then got overtaken by anger of a magnitude totally unfamiliar to me. My whole life was a lie, an illusion crushed by a truth my daughter had been carrying all her life, all alone. Having matured into a bonding member of my family, I lost belief in myself as a woman in a loving relationship with her parents. More importantly, I lost belief in myself as a good mother: a mother who loved her children more than life itself, a mother who would do anything to protect her babies, even live when she wanted to die. But I hadn't protected Holly and I couldn't fit the illusion back together. Looking at Holly's childhood pictures brought me to tears and despair. I was no longer able to see her sweet face and our life of love beyond what had been done to her. I have never felt more alone. Or panicked. I held on tightly to Bryan.

First, I had to grapple with the initial flood of violent thoughts that kept me up at night and resurfaced again and again, over and over. I thought a lot about killing her perpetrators. Cynthia said she would go with me.

I didn't return calls from my parents for a couple of months, though we had become accustomed to talking about once a week. Knowing my mother—when faced with the prospect of leaving her husband—I thought she would be afraid for herself financially and I wanted to reassure her that I would take care of her. I developed a plan to remodel the downstairs of my house so my mother could move in and have a nice space of her own. I never considered the possibility that she would not share my horror and pain, or that, difficult as Holly's revelations were to hear, she would not believe or accept as truth what I was about to tell her. Expecting her support, I called them.

My mother and "Dad" (as I had called my stepfather for years) each got on an extension phone at their home in Bellingham. All I remember now is my mother screaming that Holly's claims weren't true and using colorful language outside her norm. The two of them yelled and screamed at me, demanding I never say "that" again. Then my mother screamed, "Well, she always has been a sexy little thing!" They sexualized my baby as their defense before going back to denial.

After hanging up on me, I would learn that their next call went to my brother, Robert, the attorney. Robert gave them some questionable lawyerly advice and later told me that he thought his father's abuse was in some way racially motivated. I don't know if I didn't have the heart to explore that theory further with Robert or if I just don't want to remember the details of such a conversation. Whatever Ned's motivations, I know alcohol was involved in his abuse of Holly. By this time in my mother and Ned's marriage, a day wasn't a day without a bottle of scotch. But in my lifelong desire to be part of a loving family, I hadn't seen the potential for harm. Being a practiced, adult child of alcoholics, I'd just timed my phone calls before cocktail hour at five o'clock. I preferred to believe they really loved me and my children. Anything less was unthinkable.

As adults, I thought my siblings and I had all made it past the early years and our parents' commitment to never allow us to do or say anything to break them up. I guess none of their own behaviors would warrant them breaking up, either. I truly never envisioned my mother continuing to stay with Ned, but she did so—until he died. I'd hoped she might want to heal our relationship after he died, but she maintained her loyalty to him up to the day she died.

After those revelatory phone calls in the Spring of 1989, my entire family stopped speaking to me. I was told that Holly didn't want me to call the police or press charges or confront anyone. I don't remember those conversations or who I had them with. I'm guessing I received this information from her counselors at school. Regardless of how this request was presented to me, I regret abiding by it. Had I found the courage or received different guidance, perhaps, I would have related to my children differently and felt less pressure going forward to perpetually protect them from this mean world. Perhaps I would feel more complete, less weakened by the abuse Holly was forced to endure: violations that forever changed our lives and my relationship with my daughter, my son, my family, and my friends.

Years later, when Holly and I talked about these events, she remembered her intense desire to keep them private. Her older male cousin, Anthony, had found out about the abuse and wanted to go after the boys across the street, but she'd discouraged Anthony from acting on his intentions. She did not want him to get into trouble. She also didn't want the kids talking about her. They could be so mean at that age. She didn't want to be one of "those girls" who were judged or talked about at school, and she couldn't imagine anything beneficial coming from pressing charges—except, perhaps, more trouble.

I really had no idea what Holly needed from me, and all I had was love, anger, and a broken heart. If I had known what to do, I would have done it, then or now. I'm sure I missed things she needed, something more she wanted from me. I'm sure her counselors missed things too. I have yet to grasp how my six-year-old son understood or internalized what happened to his sister—or why her legitimate anger flowed toward me throughout his childhood and would occasionally show up in our adult relationships. I tried to navigate this sea of uncertainty and heartache and establish appropriate boundaries around and with my children without guidance—and with little support. Looking for evidence of their healing would become a lonely and private venture. I turned toward therapy, research, and a deeper spiritual inquiry, seeking a context to understand such betrayal, even to justify life as it continued to unfold. And sometimes, I still wish . . .

I Wish

I wish I had taken legal action.

I wish I had fought and held them all accountable.

I wish I had made them pay for the pain and violation they imposed on my daughter.

I wish I had put myself in front of each one and made them look at me and feel the impact of my rage.

I wish that what Holly internalized during those years, and all that she has suffered because of it, could be erased.

And with all my heart I wish for the places where Holly hides
   her pain to be healed and that the lifetime of healing work
   initiated by her courage to speak her truth contributes to the
   healing of anyone who has ever suffered because of childhood violation and abuse.
This is my forever prayer.
And so it is.

It was over a year before Robert wrote to me and sent some pictures he had taken at the house in Bellingham on a trip he made
to visit our parents. The pictures made me heartsick and angry,
but I picked up the olive branch Robert extended and we followed up with lunch. That is how Robert and I began to rebuild
trust, our friendship, and our sense of family.

   Several years passed. Ned had open heart surgery, followed by
a stroke. I thought that these events reflected his actions as well
as his inactions. For a man so out of alignment with his integrity,
it made sense that his heart would fail and a stroke would leave
him unable to speak the necessary apologies. Robert visited the
parents in Bellingham again and told me that he'd asked his father,
"If I brought Holly into this room right now, what would you say
to her?" Apparently, their discussion got heated and Ned flailed
and yelled in his post-stroke garble, "I'm sorry." He never apolo-
gized to Holly or to me. As Robert's and Ned's voices rose in
aggravation, my mother came in yelling and kicked Robert out of
the room and forbade him from seeing Ned again.

I stayed in therapy and read everything I could about childhood sexual abuse and about the parents of children who had been abused. Even in 1989, I still didn't have much to work with, but *The Courage to Heal* by Ellen Bass and Laura Davis would soon provide steppingstones toward healing and the sad realization that in this experience, I was not alone—and neither was Holly.

All seemed well with Bryan and we kept busy with his activities, school, and friends. We visited Holly on family weekends, making them into mini-vacations, until we began her transition back home midway through her junior year of high school.

Cascade School was rich and meaningful for Holly. She was among the wealthy, white, and privileged at the school and only the third Black student in the program; the first was long gone and the second had arrived the day before Holly. Holly remembers two students who came right up to her and said, "I don't understand how a Black person can get with a white person and make you." Until she'd gone to Cascade, Holly had always checked the "Other" box when a form asked her to indicate her race. Although her skin was brown, she was born to and being raised by her white mom, after all, so "Other" was the most accurate choice offered at that time. It was a Cascade counselor who'd advised her that the world would always identify her as a Black woman. On school applications, she was told, it might benefit her to make that selection instead.

Cascade didn't offer an ideal environment for her, but Holly developed many valuable life skills and had some amazing experiences through a vision quest program and quarterly intensives. To this day, she appreciates the values she was able to clarify and her time overall at Cascade. When she came home, she wanted to get on with what she called and hoped for—a "normal life." She graduated from a local private high school and moved to Los Angeles to be with her Cascade friends and break into modeling, music, and her big dreams under the auspices of attending college with my support. I found my next job and stayed busy with Bryan's activities and keeping myself together while diving into my personal work, trying to understand what is beyond understanding.

After telling my mother about Ned's violation of Holly, the first and last time I saw her again was at the wedding of my brother Bill. I wanted to be a part of what was good in Bill's life and he had invited Bryan to be in the wedding party. I began mentally and emotionally preparing to see my mother. She, by contrast, was on the plane heading for Washington, DC, with Bill and his friends before learning we would be attending.

Holly was nineteen and living in Los Angeles. I don't venture to guess what Holly's thoughts were on attending and being in her grandmother's company, but I longed for healing with my mother. Of course, Bryan knew about our family rift. But I think at eleven he was up for the trip to DC and all our other vacation activities planned for after the wedding.

The first night turned out to be fun: most of the family and friends had arrived and we met up in the hotel. Holly won the one-hundred-dollar karaoke contest and Bill's friends were thrilled to meet us. My mom was staying with friends, delaying our meeting until the next evening's rehearsal dinner. Bill and his friend invited Bryan to go with them to pick up Bryan's grandmother. Holly and I waited for them to return, futzing anxiously in our hotel room. When Bryan came back, I could see in his face that the visit with Grandma hadn't gone well, but I asked him how things went anyway. "I think she was nervous," Bryan said. "She couldn't remember my name."

On our way to the rehearsal-dinner dining room, I walked into the bar where my mother had chosen to sit first, bent down, and kissed her cheek. Holly did the same. I don't pretend to understand what our show of affection was like for Holly after being so rejected. My mother kept her head down and dug around in the purse on her lap, ostensibly looking for her cigarettes. A few minutes later, she was seated on my right at our assigned table in the dining room, Holly was on my left, and Bryan was seated at the wedding party table with Bill, the bride, and his friends. We made small talk through dinner as my mom repeatedly insisted someone bring her an ashtray, despite the no-smoking designation.

The next day's wedding was lovely. A chorus of beautiful bells played, Bryan was handsome in his tux alongside Bill and the groomsmen. I believe it was the last time I saw Bill standing on his own with just the support of a cane while he and his future wife said their vows. Bill's bride sat on his lap as they danced in his wheelchair, surrounded by friends ready to party and celebrate their joy. During the reception, Holly and I sat several tables away from my mother. Food and champagne were served. The available beverages strategically excluded scotch, my mother's drink of choice. She hated champagne and called her friends to pick her up early, not one to miss her five o'clock cocktail for any reason. I walked out to say goodbye where she was waiting for her ride, trying still to reach her. "Mom, are we ever going to talk about what happened?"

"Nothing happened!" she said in a strangled voice.

"How can you say that? It did happen. It's been almost five years since we talked, and I keep waiting. When will you stop being in denial?"

"Denial! Denial! What's that, one of your therapy words?" she spit out.

"Mom! I want to talk with you."

"There's nothing to talk about!" she shouted.

"Yes. There is!" I shouted back. Frustrated and hurt, as usual, I turned away as I began to cry. "I really don't understand you," I muttered.

"Well, you're still beautiful!" she screamed at my back. It always sounded like she hated me when she said that. When I turned and looked at her face, my suspicions were confirmed.

We spoke one more time after that. I called her when Ned died a couple years later. The conversation was brief. She thanked me for the call and the distance remained, despite my long-held fantasy that when Ned died, she might open to me with a reconsidered measure of honesty and heart. I have always believed she knew the truth. Once again—and I wish I could say finally—the illusion of my mother's capacity to love me and my children collapsed.

Ned died in January 1994. Bernice died in June 2003. They were married twenty-eight years. At the end of their lives, Barb was the only one of six children who remained of interest or in their favor. After our mother was diagnosed with cancer, I was told that Barb quickly had a new will drawn up and moved our mother to a hospital bed in her living room.

Barb let everyone know Mom was dying. Neither Robert nor I accepted her invitation to visit. Bill was able to see Mom only once because there was no wheelchair access to Barb's house. Jim flew to Seattle to see Mom. He told me that he thanked Bernice for taking such good care of his dad. Hearing those words of appreciation, she opened her eyes from an apparent near-death state and looked at him with recognition. Barb attended to Mom's brief end-of-life needs, changed the title on our parents' house, and claimed all that belonged to their years of marriage and world travel. Maybe she felt she had earned her inheritance and paid the price for being the one child who remained loyal to the lie. Or maybe it was more than that. My inheritance was an obligatory one thousand dollars, one framed photo, and one brown mug, reflective of my sister's distribution of assets. (The photo was a black-and-white of me at about five. I had made the brown mug in Girl Scouts and carved with a toothpick *Barb, Billy and Me* around the outside.)

Since then, my sister and I have never bridged the gap. During my mother's brief illness, Barb wrote several letters to Robert and Jim, which they shared with me. The condescending and critical feelings she held toward me echoed the hatred and disdain she had expressed in her threatening phone call when she invited me to see my mother before she died. Barb was still protecting the lie of Ned's innocence and insisting that if I came to see Mom, I was not to mention Holly's name or anything that might upset her. My stomach cramped and nausea filled my body; the sound of Barb's voice was like a punch in the stomach. Though I foolishly longed for some sense of recognition, love, and closure with my mother, I decided against putting myself once again within striking distance of Barb. I didn't see my mother before she died, and I have yet to see or speak again with my sister.

My parents' inability to love their children was baffling—even more so to Robert, Jim, Cappy, and me as we became parents ourselves. They'd always parented from a place of duty rather than heart, and once they were done, they had no interest in any of their grandchildren, either. They missed the opportunity to explore what a loving family could be or to show us that life is strengthened by loving one another or to let us know that it was safe to be ourselves. Only room for two—plus one willing to swear her undying loyalty—in my parents' universe.

Family Love's Finale

Bill's marriage ended in divorce after a few years. I continue to be in Bill's life. I call him every few days. pay his cell phone bill, serve as his health and personal advocate when needed, send chocolate-covered fruit, flowers occasionally, and something to cheer up his room at Christmas. I fly to visit and lend a hand now and then and give money less frequently than I once did. He has been in a nursing home since he was sixty and no longer able to live independently. To me, the most remarkable thing about Bill is how deeply he values his life. After being born with cerebral palsy and enduring many subsequent medical conditions, Bill's life has been both complicated and blessed by many surgeries and medical specialists. As he aged, he faced many new challenges. And yet many people with far fewer problems than Bill scarcely appreciate their life circumstances. I am always amazed by his spirit.

I am sorry that my mother didn't anticipate and prepare for his later-in-life needs. She could have done better by him, but she didn't. Some of that responsibility rests at my sister's feet. Apparently, she decided my mother had given Bill enough money during his life. Through the years, Barb's running competition with Bill for which sibling was the neediest or most deserving became a raw source of entertainment for Robert and me.

Robert and I remained close until his sudden death in September 2021. We reexamined our family relations many times, but mostly we talked of love, friendship, God, and our relationship with the angels. His certainty was so grounding and reassuring. I miss him.

Jim died surprisingly in June 2023. Cappy thinks Jim's death was caused by his sadness over losing Robert. She has a large family and lives in Israel, in terrifying circumstances. The war and our

distance from each other is a factor, but love and her significance
in my heart travel easily.

Jim's death initiated a spiral of grief over the next twelve
months that grew to include the deaths of four more beloveds,
Lu, Andee, Marilyn, and Marilyn's husband, Bob.

Before

Before I knew about heartbreak, betrayal, and death,
I lived in a joy-filled place,
partially of my own creation.
The air was fresh and the streamers on my bike
snapped in the wind as I rode down the hill,
past the boys in the street ready
to toss the dead snake they were messing with,
hoping to mess with me.

I could have known sooner.
Before the wind in my hair grew still.
Before my cat was hit by a car.
Before they gave away my dog without telling me.

Before the phone rang and life changed with the news.
Daddy's plane had crashed in the Mojave Desert.
The Condor they collided with had died too.
Before I knew my mother wouldn't talk to me for years
in defense of her next husband.

Before I twisted myself into a girl that a boy not worthy of my
    seventeen-year-old mind and body might want.
Someone to make a good wife at eighteen.
Someone less challenging, someone less happy.

Before my loves died of cancer leaving me to raise our beautiful
biracial children in a world struggling to right its wrongs and
live up to a better promise.
Before I knew love could transform and evaporate and its absence break your heart or drag you lower than you'd ever
imagined.

Before I knew that with the years I might lose hope in humanity
and some days myself.
Before I knew I could climb out of the darkness and release my
body back to the wind to begin again.

Before you give up
run wild
write wild
explore your interior wilderness.
Be generous with your love, even before you think you have
enough to give away.

Do all this before you let go.
It might surprise you before your final goodbye.

Love Nurtures Beauty

The creation of beauty in my home once again became my focus.
My home is my palette, the place where my artistry first began to
show up and the place it continues to express itself most freely.
My new house was on a double lot with trees of many varieties:
pines and old oaks, oranges and apricots, figs and camellias. Early
on, I had a half-court basketball court installed at the far end of
the backyard with a dog run alongside it. The yard was a constant

work in progress, becoming more and more beautiful with the help of a landscape-designer friend and her team of rock-moving, hole-digging sons.

Over the years, gardens and water features filled in the mid-portion—ferns and ginger flowers, creeping purple flowers and wild white iris, benches and boulders offered luscious places to seek peace and serenity. Quan Yin, the Chinese goddess of mercy, graced the edge of the pond and a bamboo fountain added to the soundtrack of growing comfort. Repeatedly, however, I needed to supply the pond with fish and fresh lilies, thanks to my destructive little friends, the raccoons. Those pesky critters ate the fish and oranges every night leaving fingernail-size bits of peel and half-eaten oranges all over the pea gravel and plants surrounding the pond. Over and over, they tossed the bamboo fountain spout and dismantled the stones carefully designed to hide the mechanical equipment. I tried every possible remedy to discourage them . . . to no avail. Finally, I placed pictures of raccoons over my home office desk and prayed to the Raccoon Diva, hoping to find a peaceful resting place outside each morning. Instead, I started my day by cleaning up after those rascals.

Creating beautiful spaces and view spots is a joyful pursuit for me. I invite my sources of inspiration and welcome their arrival. The process of creating a new vision with what I already have is not only a great way to shift my energy but is also extremely satisfying. It's a reset button I can hit as often as I like. Then I can relax in beauty, until the next time I become restless in my space or my body and arise alongside the muse to move things around again. Perhaps the rascally raccoons invaded my territory to keep me ever on my toes, connected to beauty. Today, the squirrels on my patio are my nemeses.

ACT V

Love Seeks Connection

After GB died, I remember the first moment I wasn't in pain. It had been six or maybe eight months and I was at the movies with Cynthia, my soul-sister bestie. She was my Saturday night "date" for over a year until I told her she really needed a new boyfriend, and happily it wasn't long before Dave showed up in her life. But meanwhile, we were at the movies one night watching *Moonstruck*, with Cher and Nicolas Cage. This new sensation came without forewarning. Just a pinpoint of light that penetrated me in a dark theater. In that tiny speck of light for an inexplicable moment I felt no pain and my mind was quiet. That was the moment I built upon. That was the moment I thought my survival might be possible. Perhaps I could survive the pain of losing GB, myself, and the life of love I thought I had been shepherding all along as mother to my beloved children, embraced by a family that loved us. I had no clear road map but a mysterious new sense of possibility.

Five years after GB died, my beloved friend Cynthia died of cancer. As she was preparing to leave this world, she looked toward the corner of her bedroom—surrounded by her children and the husband of her heart, Dave—and said, "GB is here. Do you see him?" This memory of Cynthia brings me joy, even now. I miss her and think of her often. I could write a book about our conversations and all the reasons she was loved. One of Cynthia's unique qualities was that most people who knew her remembered the exact moment they connected with her. I find that rare! For one friend it was when he learned that she had been a *Jeopardy!* contestant as a young mother of three and grew instantly impressed and curious about her. My moment happened when we were first getting to know each other and she shared that she had also dated Black men. It opened a new level of trust between us, a safe space in which I had no fear of racism showing up unexpectedly.

I built a new life with my children in a home that I loved and felt safe in. Some local events got our attention for a while, like the 1989 Loma Prieta earthquake and the 1991 Oakland Hills fire, along with the house behind us burning down, sparks flying dangerously close to the huge pine tree in our backyard. Bryan was a good kid, busy with school, friends, and after-school activities and largely trying to do the right thing and not cause his mom any more trouble. World events were barely on my radar until the Rodney King verdict allowed the four white police officers accused in his brutal beating to walk free. That news rocked the nation and my world in terrifying and confusing ways. The day after the verdict, Bryan and I walked down our street to the video store and some unknown Black teens sitting on their porch threw rocks at us. Racial tensions were visible and once again running high. I checked out holistic healing practices, churches, and courses of spiritual study. I stayed in therapy, enrolled Bryan in the Big Brothers program, and at one point, found him a therapist. I wanted to be sure he had a safe man to talk with and I didn't want to miss a thing that could harm him. The latter was an impossible mission, but I remained vigilant regardless.

Friends were a big part of my life and I continued to be blessed with many. Men came and went—a pattern that had little impact but was nice while I was in the throes of new possibility. Most notably, for about the first fifteen years after GB's death, I stayed busy. I worked hard and had a busy professional, social, and family life, and with my many girlfriends, life was fun, entertaining, and fulfilling. I continued to meditate, walk, study, and search for spiritual understanding and a context for containing a life of loss. But in the rearview mirror, I see unattended sorrow, despite my attempt to stabilize and stay focused on ways to live and care for Holly and Bryan. It would take years before I regained my personal strength and sense of self.

About the time that GB died, the parents of Holly's friend Tiffany were getting a divorce. Holly and Tiffany had met at Shakespeare Camp at Oakland's Holy Names University the summer they were eleven and spent a lot of time together. As "responsible" parents, whenever we dropped the girls off for an afternoon or overnight at each other's houses, we would often stop to chat for a few minutes. Through those brief exchanges, we liked each other but hadn't become personal friends just yet. One Saturday afternoon, I went to the door with Holly to say hello before leaving her there. Tiffany's mother, Gwen, was just making lunch and offered me a tuna sandwich. Sitting in her sunny living room, we bonded that afternoon and became single mothers together and inseparable friends.

Over time, our families and friends intertwined and we shared holidays and feasts for years. We were each committed to our kids, their education and well-being, we both worked full-time, and we both loved sharing and entertaining in the beauty of our homes. We went to jazz clubs, dancing, shopping, and shows, Paris and Brazil, and weekend getaways with girlfriends and sometimes boyfriends. We always seemed to be having fun. These occasions were a big part of my life and survival. Gwen's spontaneity and style buoyed me. I was available and my presence didn't take away from her stardom.

Gwen became my daily adviser and first point of contact with any problem, relationship, idea, or concern. With the exception of work, I didn't make any decisions without her input, and I usually acted on her clear and steadfast advice. Gradually, however, I came to realize that I had unwittingly been following Gwen's counsel without first consulting my own feelings and inner guidance. Neither of us seemed to notice that parts of me were absent. I lived in denial about just how broken, sad, and alone I felt. Instead, I coasted, numb inside, preferring to put a smile on my face and rely on Gwen's way of moving through the world. Our friendship suited us most of the time, but eventually, I had to find my way back to myself. I ventured toward reconnecting with my own authority and authenticity. Some distance developed between us, then I wrote Gwen a letter explaining how I felt. She never responded to the letter and that chapter of our friendship closed without another conversation.

It would be years, and as a consequence of the death of her son, that Gwen and I would be back in each other's lives again. When I heard the terrible news, I didn't hesitate to call Gwen and fly to California to be with the family. Love can be inexplicable in its nature to survive distances, differences, and time.

Love Closures

Seeing Frank's name in my email inbox one day a few years ago gave me a sliver of curiosity. My interest dulled upon realizing that some professional app neither one of us was all that engaged in had auto-generated the email in response to a birthday reminder. But there he was. And once, we had been engaged. And I remembered. Despite having burned my journals shortly after we met, I remembered—the good, the bad, and the really small, painful ways that our beautiful sense of new love had turned into pain, anger, and sadness.

The good: new love is fun and brings alive those who dare to tango with it. In the beginning, we lived together really well. We liked coming home to each other. We figured out finances, family, cooking, and house projects. We did well parenting our young sons together. His youngest son, Michael, was with us most weekends and Bryan lived the day-to-day with us, adjusting to his mom being in a full-on relationship with a new man. (A big difference from having a single mom who dates and only occasionally makes an introduction to her son.) Blending a family is a growth experience for both kids and parents. I deeply appreciated watching Bryan and Michael become friends and make the best of our family merger. Occasionally devious, they pranked us and each other, adding to the laughter in our home. Frank and his family had a positive and inclusive influence on Bryan as well as Holly, who was living at the time in Los Angeles. I carry sweet memories and gratitude for the good times.

I loved Frank when wine and candlelight, love and lust had us dancing naked in the dining room. I loved Frank in the summer, camping and boating with all his manly competencies on display. I loved him and prayed for him to stay safe every day at work and I loved the way he promised to come home to me each night.

The bad: Against my better judgment, I hired the girlfriend of one of his older sons to work in my office and things immediately started going south. Another son scammed me in a pyramid game without regret or apology. Frank told his mother he probably would have cheated on me had we not broken up. She told me about his revelation over lunch later. I think she was trying to help me see that the breakup was a good thing.

The worst: into our second year together, I didn't feel cared for or valued. I longed for Frank to apply his professional skills to his love for me: to protect, defend, and deescalate when it came to his sons, but we could no longer communicate. I couldn't understand his words or the order in which they came from his lips. I began wondering what I had been hearing the first eight months that I could no longer hear. In my confusion, I still loved him.

After I burned my journals, we lived together for about a year and a half. We got engaged, bought a Corvette, had some fun, and discovered all the reasons not to stay together. Within a few months after our first breakup, we got back together and broke up again soon after that.

The end.

A Temporary Love

When writing a love story, the images can change.
How we remember a love gone sour
    can become poetic and kind once again.
Or not.
Once upon a time, I loved you.
Once upon a time, you loved me.
It didn't last as long as we expected.
It was a normal breakup, I guess, though I have little experience
    in such things.
A realization
A decision

A choice for change
A move
Goodbye. Like that.

I suspect normal breakups can be thoughtful. A simple letting go when you can't figure out how to like being together anymore. No need to villainize. But breakups don't usually go that way. People struggle with the details of a separation and who made who the most miserable. It hurts. I wish endings weren't that way and I admire those who figure out how to make the transition with love.

The anger, disappointment, and powerful longing I felt at the end of my relationship with Frank was internal: uncomfortable, an inexplicable attachment I couldn't shake. Painful new places opened within me that were beyond Frank's capacity to deal with, leading me to seek a deeper level of healing than I had achieved before his arrival. I compared to him each new man who came along after that, hoping to feel safe and open again, happy and trusting like I had been when Frank and I first met.

In the aftermath, I hurt others by being unavailable and over-looked a few more men who cared. I played around the edges of other romantic loves that followed and embraced what came. In love, as with most everything, I feel and listen for a yes. But when a no turns up, I pay attention.

One day, while walking around Lake Merritt, I would come across a man who said, "I know you!"

The man who said he knew me happened to be clutching the other side of a dollar bill I'd stopped to offer him. He was sitting on the street with a notebook and a cup in hand. I looked into his eyes, past the shabby plaid jacket, dusty knit cap, and sorry lines on his face. I released the bill and he held it in the air midway to his pocket.

He was a man I knew to be a poet, brilliant with words, handsome, intense, lyrical, and kind, and a bit of a train wreck—even years earlier, when we first met. But I am a woman who appreciates a poetic heart—the uniqueness of the individual—and I'm forgiving. He was a man who loved garden roses and once stole a full and fragrant bouquet for me from his neighbor's yard. (I always wished he hadn't told me about the stealing part.) He taught me to cook mushrooms to a chewy perfection using soy sauce and introduced me to green-lipped mussels at a Chinese restaurant. He was a man who brought me antique linen napkins from a barn sale in Wisconsin when he returned to Berkeley after caring for his dad as he was dying. He was a man who first explained intimacy to me: *In-to-me-see!* And I did. He was a man who fell hard while young, a man who tried to get clean and create a life he could love. A man who wanted to be the man he knew I deserved.

He intended to do me a favor and drop my car off at the body shop. Instead, he kept it for two days, fell off the wagon, and one of my office staff saw him with a woman in the front seat of my unmistakable 1963 Cadillac convertible. Head hung low in the position of shame that only a dog or an addict can hold, he returned my car. Shame seeped from his eyes, the color of his skin: once brown and full, now gray and hollow.

He was a man whose picture and poetry I tore up when he let me down.

Many years had passed by the time I saw him on the street and those years had not been kind to him.

Those part-time, every-once-in-a-while men were generally not good fits for me. I explored relationships with them with hope and possibility and could occasionally feel an attraction to some aspect of their hearts, but I never fully connected again. Many wounded men live in the world who, by no surprise, go on to meet wounded women. Some seek fun, others sex, and some are actually searching for a true connection—just as I was. A lot of sorting out had to be done in the world of dating, not to mention navigating the complex new world of online introductions. Yep, I kissed a few frogs, hoping for another prince or, even better, an interesting, fun, and kind-hearted man with a long and loving life ahead.

In a church sermon I heard during that time, a minister said, "Everyone is walking around wanting to attract a ten, but they're functioning at the level of a two. It doesn't work that way! You have to be the love at the level you wish to attract." So, I worked on myself and moved beyond the repetitious disappointment associated with dating.

Love and the Path of Depression

I wanted a deeper connection. I called it love, I called it God, I called it a new man—but, as mentioned, a few of those men came and went. Often, I didn't know what to call my longing beyond an emptiness within myself that ached to be filled but remained hollow. I struggled through a fog of confusion—with loss being my repetitious teacher—and I continued to seek a personal understanding in which to frame my experience. And I went to work, where I could focus and feel creative and some semblance of control. Through those years of staying busy, I thought I would move through my period of grief and then get on with my life and maybe a new man. Create a life I could love again. But time, the great healer, had a surprise for me. Grief teaches, and while it does change, it can never be forgotten. Once grief tears us open, it sinks into our hearts, reconnecting us to the love that once drew us to our lost beloveds—the source of our essential love within.

I went through the five stages according to Elisabeth Kübler-Ross: denial, anger, bargaining, depression, and acceptance—only to discover a cycle: wash, rinse, repeat! The cycle occurs when someone dies or we lose a job, a friend, a home, an image of ourselves, our sense of security or position in life, our health and vitality, even our youth (aging being its own particular teacher, I'm learning). According to Stephen Levine, as we are cycling through the five stages, we are passing from hell into heaven. The five stages can be seen as a path to unblock our "original nature" rather than our reality. These mind-changing moments can bring awareness to the one certainty in life: everything will change. It's all temporary. That is how my days were going: mind opening and closing moment to moment, tear by tear, fear by fear, in between the laughter, time with friends, and my unwavering love for Holly and Bryan.

Depression, Deep Sorrow, and Grief

Depression is a disconnection from your spirit, your essence,
> and your purpose.
Difficult to grasp when your body will not move and your mind
> is too tired to care.
Down where the deep sorrow lives, grief is longing to find ex-
> pression and a deeper peace.
Deep sorrow is different from depression.
It's where grief resides until life ceases to require
> that it be ignored, tamped down, and swallowed
So life can be fulfilled as a parent, a professional,
> a family member and friend, a student and spiritual seeker,
> teacher and mentor,
A woman who makes decisions, buys cars and houses, art and
> jewelry, plane tickets and vacations, furniture and flowers,
Employs gardeners, painters, and housekeepers,
Pays tuition and prays to the Racoon Diva
> as she curses and rebuilds the koi pond each morning
> in the garden where she had planned to meditate.

ACT VI

The First Day of Belonging

Spiritual teachings offer the belief that each day is the first day: renewed, mystical, and magically free, forgiven, and beyond yesterday's struggle.

I have not held these teachings to be an absolute truth, although they do inspire a certain gentle acceptance. An invitation to hit the reset button and grow wings. To imagine being the hawk on the top of the pine tree appearing calm amid the murderous crows—your heart pounding reminds you of your aliveness.

The first day of life in the woods, sleek and strong, cat-like with four legs and calloused paws quietly moving over the soft, moist bed of pine needles, imagining the leap it will take to catch what your senses have not yet been alerted to, but ready all the same.

The first day of life underwater, tons of you moving with sonic guidance and grace. Then a sudden surge drives you to break the surface, catch the onlooker's eye, and fall back into the deep, tail wide, slapping as you dive, taking the heart-stopping moment with you.

The first day as the tree itself. The one the hawk perches in just above the crow's nest, the one that so generously drops her needles to carpet the earth, the one you have watered with your tears that filled the rivers that run to the sea. The tree you lean against to ground yourself into the imaginary world of the first day.

The tree whose strength lets you know you are essential, connected to all that is.

Love Changes Her Name

I tried on my former name in the early morning minutes of just waking. I missed that name, or was it "her" that I missed, as I sometimes do? Kris Johnson-Ayers. I try the name on like clothing now and then, an outfit hanging in the back of the closet that for a time didn't fit, then got replaced.

Deep into my spiritual journey in the late '90s, I began thinking about changing my last name. My children were hovering around adulthood and anchoring into their own lives. It was time to try yet another path to freeing myself from grief and attachment to the past. I was searching for a new level of resonance, a way to become me without my name forever linked to my two dead husbands. Changing my name was symbolic for me, if inconvenient for a few old friends and family members, some who still haven't been able to update their operating systems.

I believe a name matters. To parents, the naming of a child is usually given thoughtful consideration. When I got pregnant with my daughter, I was working on the maternity floor at Children's Hospital in San Francisco. She was to be born in November and one of the nurses suggested the name Holly, since her birth would be during the holiday season. I loved it. Symbolically, Holly means "sacred" and represents a courageous and optimistic nature with a lucky number of six. She was born November 6! Bryan was named after his father, whose full legal name was "GB"—just the initials. We'd entertained ourselves with lists of names that began with a G followed by a B. (No one had more fun than my Auntie June, who addressed cards to GB at the hospital using her latest comedic suggestion and giving the mailroom staff something to twitter about. Seriously—Graham Bonaparte?) We began calling the baby Bryan, and when our son was about three months old, we finalized his first name, choosing Geoffrey, meaning "divine peace." Bryan means "strong and honorable." Both children have lived up to their ascribed characteristics.

Having no heart-connection to my maiden name—and consistent with the times—I had changed my last name with all three marriages, hyphenating the last two to maintain name connection with both children. In the late '70s, I had read the novel *Meridian* by Alice Walker. This beautifully written story of pain, love, and possibility made a powerful impact, and I found the name of the main character magnetic. If I had another daughter, I thought, I would name her "Meridian." But my son was born next and last. As a name, I continued to consider "Meridian" compelling. I began testing it out for restaurant reservations. When I heard the host call out "Meridian," each syllable sounded like music. It took me another year to decide upon my last name. After a year of research and meditation, Tibetan numerological calculations of every consideration, and energy and angel consultations through friends and spirit guides, I chose "Kristi," my childhood first name. The meanings I live by include freedom-loving and free-spirited: nothing conventional, given my life of change and adventure. In Alice Walker's novel of the same name, she defines "Meridian" as a high point of development, power, or prosperity, the prime of life, the highest point a celestial body travels, as midday, and as one of the energy pathways in the body in accordance with traditional Chinese medicine.

I claimed the energy of the noonday sun and embraced myself with the strength of Meridian.

In 2001, as part of my every-once-in-a-while Christmas letter, I wrote about the way Native American and other world cultures understand that our names carry power, shape our identity, support us in who and how we are to be, and accompany us into our fullest expression. I wrote of my love and appreciation for my birth name, chosen by my parents, and thanked the men whose names I had accepted when we'd married. I wrote about my year focused on healing my heart through spiritual growth in Mastery of the Heart school and the crack in the heart of the world that September 11 created. I wrote about raising five thousand dollars for the Leukemia & Lymphoma Society and the benefits and blisters earned by walking the Portland Marathon September 30, 2001. (Early post-9/11, just getting on a plane and leaving the Bay Area felt like an act of bravery.) I finished walking the marathon with the honorable completion time of six hours, thirty-eight minutes, and twenty seconds.

I wrote this short poem and trimmed my announcement with a holiday border and marathon finish line photos.

Meridian Kristi

A spirit freeing itself to expand and experience new life.
Free and soaring to vistas previously unexplored,
Viewing the night sky with eyes that have never before seen
    stars so bright,

Greeting the day with a loving heart and a mind learning to be
    silent.
Creating from love
Ahhh, blessed peace.

Eddie and GB, I discovered, are inextricably part of me, regardless of my name. They remain forever in my heart and mind,
woven as strong threads in the tapestry of my life. I see them in
Holly and Bryan and they visit my dreams. They guide and protect
me, influence and inform me, and always speak lovingly. I am
grateful my life has included them across the divide.

War Loves No One

War, Still, and Again: March 19, 2003
On the Invasion of Iraq

Fear in my body. I am awake.
I am the witness, afraid of what the day will hold.
Afraid to turn on the news. Afraid to face what we've done.
Another atrocity to overcome. More white guilt and arrogance
    to process.
How do I accept that we are all one, connected, and creative—
    yet killing is our native response?

Where is the peace?

My heart feels pain that I watch travel to my head, where the top
closes quickly like a drawstring purse.
Reverse.
Constriction moving downward, now to the base of my spine,
reaching round, filling my belly, and drawing my legs up at
the hips.
Ears suddenly alert, mind rapidly seeking the truth of this morning through the fragile sensitivities of a newly awakened body
and the thirty-sixth hour of war in Iraq.

I feel the attack as I reach across the world in prayer.
People are dying, suffering indignities too great to imagine.
My body is hypervigilant to the blow I know is coming.
Where is the peace?

Going within, again, I scan my body for a clue.
Stomach hard, neck and shoulders twisted.
The war has begun in my body.
I cough to expel the foul taste.

Despairing in the pain of the world, I hear Mother Earth cry
out.
My body remembers war, some during my lifetime and others
I've carried with me from before.
Scanning the confusion, I feel the thick, dripping fog over a field
of sharp branches centuries old.
Gripping, groping, fearful for humanity, with insanity so close,
helpless tears arise.

But for the heart, this mind would close in on itself for lack of
understanding.

"I love you," I tell it, while longing for some soft, gentle nurtur-
ance, the warmth of the bed and a lover's reassurance.
"Oh, my heart! Keeper of the light, center of the physical and
emotional universe, find the Peace in us all.
Heal the war within us.
Let us love one another."

In the quiet, I come upon Faith and the knowing presence of
God.
My heart is beating just the same on this day, as if all it knows is
beauty.
The songbirds are singing outside my bedroom. I notice their el-
egance.
Perhaps that noticing is the best I can offer humanity today.
I rest a moment longer and find peace.

Love Heals and Then . . .

On the one-year anniversary of my mother's death—June 3,
2004—I left town on a road trip. Bryan had just completed his
associate degree and was back home from college. He was happy
to stay and take care of our pets. I had recently completed an intense, seven-year tenure as the practice administrator for a
veterinary surgical practice. I'd spent years parlaying my natural
eye for beauty and functional use of space into managing the design and construction of medical offices and surgery centers. New
business cards in hand, I was now developing a business plan to
offer my services as a construction project manager and owner-

representative. I was ready to go out on my own. This road trip was my break before diving in: a rare gift to myself.

I had a heal-that-mother-wound trip in mind. My ultimate destination would be Bellingham, Washington, my mother's hometown and the final roost for her and Ned after they retired in 1975. I drove 279 miles north on I-5 to soak and surrender for a few days at Stewart Mineral Springs in Weed, California. There, I bathed in ancient, stained claw-foot tubs filled with hot mineral-spring water, plunged in the cold river, enjoyed a massage or two, and slept in a rustic, rickety, cabin-style room on the property. I spent hours writing to allow my feelings to float to the surface where I could explore them and then consider the next leg of my trip. For years to come, I would return to Stewart's for sweat lodges and ceremonies.

My next stop was Ashland, Oregon, then Portland, followed by Seattle and Bellingham. Along the way, I visited friends and family and enjoyed the scenery, the drive, and the quiet. I practiced not thinking about work or what was ahead as the Beatles song "Let It Be" played in my mind.

Arriving in Bellingham, I continued my quest to nurture my beleaguered body and spirit. Bellingham nourished and embraced me—a place that held fond memories of family visits but where in 1989, my mother and sister had expelled me from their lives.

First, I checked into the beautiful Chrysalis Inn and Spa, then walked over to explore all that was new and gentrified in Fairhaven, Bellingham's historic and once-familiar neighborhood. I bought myself a large bouquet of white, long-stemmed roses to adorn my room. This time, I wrote poetry and prose on a window seat above the railroad tracks overlooking Bellingham Bay. The train rolled by periodically, the sound oddly soft and reminiscent of the faraway train in my childhood memories of San Mateo. I drove around town, past the houses of my maternal grandparents, Auntie Tina, and my mother. Barb—whom I hadn't seen or spoken to in the year since Mom died—now owned my mother's home and was renting it as an absentee landlord. Her tenant welcomed me in and showed me around. I was flooded with memories and grateful for the tenant's kindness. The next time I would see that house was after my sister sold it. Overgrown and dark, it seemed to reflect our family relationships: deteriorated and left behind.

I continued my stay in Fairhaven for a few days, luxuriating in another massage at the hotel spa and enjoying a couple of lovely solo meals in the hotel dining room, where in June the sun didn't fully set on the bay until after ten.

Heading south—anticipating the trip home—I retraced my drive down I-5 until I set out on a side adventure with a funny idea in the back of my head. How about buying a houseboat on the Columbia River in Portland? This consideration held great romance. Dirt cheap, by California standards. Besides, I had always loved the water and boats. Houseboats with flowerpots and vine-covered trellises, tinkling wind chimes and furnished patios, efficient but lovely and workable, tri-level living spaces—perfect. But it was cold and gray in Portland. And more than one person told me it would be freezing on a boat, even with cozy fireplaces on the lower level under the water.

Driving on, I stayed another couple of nights in Ashland and Jacksonville, enjoying the wine country and a Herbie Hancock and Wayne Shorter concert at the Britt outdoor amphitheater. There, I stood enchanted by the generosity of a place that allowed non-ticket holders to stand outside the shoulder-high fence and watch the stage. Neighbors sat in their lawn chairs, glasses of wine in hand, soaking in the live music without a ticket and—even more amazing—without complaining about the noise. I continued south the next day to the home of my friends, Rick and Dolores, an hour and a half away in Mount Shasta.

As always happens when Dolores and I adventure together (or even have a lengthy phone call), we find our way off the beaten path and into a land of the mystical and magical, opening doors to unexpected healing and insight. While walking through the downtown shops and galleries, we saw a sign taped in a store window that said ANGEL READINGS. *Right up our alley*, I thought. We called for appointments and let the magic begin.

As we got out of the car, the woman greeting us said to me, "You're from down south, right?"

"Yes," I said. "Bay Area."

"Not for long," she said as she turned to guide us up a lush stone path to a yurt near flowing water.

Dolores and I each had a reading that afternoon and left in a daze. We went home to find that Rick had prepared for the debriefing of our adventure, having placed notepaper and pens, champagne glasses, and a bottle of Veuve Clicquot on their dining room table. He was always supporting our mystical curiosities. In mulling over our readings, we wondered if we'd entered through an invisible portal that afternoon: a few days later, the path, the flowing creek, and the yurt were gone—and the angel reader along with them.

After sharing coffee and a sense of awe with Rick and Dolores the next morning, I drove back to Ashland feeling the truth of the angel reading revelation: "Your heart wants to live in Ashland." Two weeks later, after a single open house, I sold my house in Oakland. It literally sold that fast—with multiple offers. That was the spirit of the 2004 housing market and the beauty of my home. I signed the paperwork and drove back up to Ashland at 3:00 a.m., excited and sleepless. I perused properties for a couple of days and settled on a sweet house on Orange Avenue. Two major selling points: the train tracks that ran just on the other side of the back fence and the three deer napping in the open backyard under a large pussy willow tree. My heart had found a new home.

Love Rests in Beauty

Before moving into the house on Orange Avenue, I erected a fence around the yard with the illusion I could contain Codi, my single-minded Border Collie-Schipperke. After attending to this practical task, I would spend the next four and a half years landscaping and creating beauty there. The property was bountiful, laden with apple, pear, and cherry trees, a large patch of delicious heirloom raspberries, and many surprise pop-up plantings, including the most beautiful peach-colored peony I'd ever seen. I added a rose-and-lavender garden, lilies, a wide variety of flowering plants and pots, art pieces, a hot tub, fountains, a gazing ball, wind chimes—and from my Oakland garden—I brought my Quan Yin statue. I delighted in the hummingbirds, occasional cardinals, and other winged ones who came to feed and enjoy the beauty. While I was out watering most mornings, I waved at the train engineers as they slowly passed by. In winter, I lay back in the snow, scissoring my arms and legs into snow angels at three in the morning, the stars as my witness.

Once I'd settled into my new home, I realized just how burned-out I was. The move, fifteen years' work at my last two medical practices, my constantly busy lifestyle, and single parenting in the wake of grief had all caught up with me. Even my healing work seemed to have contributed to my exhaustion. The depth of my heartache still lived in me—just behind my smile and the effort I put into maintaining my fragile, positive outlook. I needed to rest.

Ashland, thankfully, was a great place to rest. From the end of February through October, tourists flocked to its great restaurants, shopping, wineries, and world-renowned theater. I was also told that for the many spiritual seekers and others intent on creating a new life, more churches, healers, and spiritual explorers existed per capita in Ashland than almost any place else on the planet. Polite attendants approached your car at the gas station and. yes—pumped your gas. And there was no traffic! (Locals cautioned me about the traffic I'd encounter while traveling across town between two and three in the afternoon. I soon learned that traffic meant five cars picking up kids in front of the elementary school.) You could park within a block of the movie theater, if not right across the street, and even the post office and Department of Motor Vehicle workers were friendly, welcoming, and happy to serve. In winter, the local population numbered about twenty thousand, and you could walk into any restaurant without a reservation. I seemed to have found the perfect place to slow down the pace of my life.

I worked my way through Julia Cameron's *The Artist's Way*, with the help of a coach named Connie and took some drawing classes with Charu, an enchanting senior woman and local artist I enjoyed getting to know. I attended evening lectures at the Rogue Valley Metaphysical Library, had a few innocuous dates, and shopped in the renowned hippie food co-op for groceries. I walked with Codi in Lithia Park, slipping my feet into the creek while she frolicked in and out of the cool, rushing water; we hiked and met new friends everywhere we went.

I walked into the bookstore on Main Street. Halfway down the aisle on the left, a book fell from the shelf onto the floor at my feet: *Unattended Sorrow*, the most recent book written by my first spiritual teacher, Stephen Levine. Another good sign from the universe! One that took my breath away.

I got a part-time job in a home decor store where I felt like the "keeper of the light" each morning as I walked around the shop turning on its many distinctive lamps. The soft light and beauty set the tone for the day as I counted my blessings and good fortune. Indeed, every day felt like Christmas as I opened boxes full of beautiful items along with my coworkers, Chris and Marsha, and set up gorgeous displays and "little altars everywhere." Fun as it was to work amid such whimsy, the store was no career move: I spent way more than I made, even with my employee discount.

I'd left my stable position as a health administrator to follow my passion. This included starting a new business parlaying my project management skills into home decorating, color, redesign, and staging. Launching Meridian Visions—Interiors Inspired by Love became an unqualified joy. I was doing what I loved most—decorating homes! In true Meridian fashion, I spent a fortune on the must-be-perfect website with music and scrolling visuals of past design projects, many of them in my friends' homes and my own, adding client homes as my business grew. My logo design and business cards were also works of art. I joined and started networking and mastermind groups, Toastmasters, and the Chamber of Commerce, and did everything I could to build my business. I loved channeling my organizational development knowledge and business experience into my own creation, and I loved meeting other creative thinkers, entrepreneurs: people willing to work toward their dreams. Many of the friends I met while living in Ashland would continue to enrich my life. Others enhanced the moments we spent working and playing together. I'm grateful I followed my heart.

Love Transitions

When I left Oakland to move to Ashland, I continued the path of spiritual exploration. I was already in my second year of practitioner training in the Church of Religious Science, aka Science of Mind (SOM), now known as the Center for Spiritual Living. I found a church in nearby Medford and went to check it out, intending to resume my course work. Over the years, I had been attending and taking foundational classes early on at the Church of Religious Science at several locations in Oakland. When the Mastery of the Heart School closed in 2001, I began taking more advanced classes.

SOM defined a practitioner as "a person of high spiritual consciousness and deep understanding who is trained in the art, science, and the skill of Spiritual Mind Treatment," a five-stage form of affirmative prayer. The practitioner essentially works with clients as a spiritual coach and "personal prayer warrior." I saw this role as a fulfilling addition to my personal and professional life. Through this form of non-denominational teaching—diverse in Eastern and Western tradition and philosophy—my spiritual understanding continued to deepen and expand.

I was in my last year of training before licensure. In Medford, I attended a few classes and church services, but I soon realized the minister just wasn't going to be my next spiritual teacher. I did, however, feel a connection with Sharie, a woman I'd requested as my prayer partner on that first night of class. The minister, however, chose not to pair me with Sharie, and I did not continue the course. But God had another idea.

One Sunday, I went to church and heard a minister I knew from his visits to my Oakland churches. He'd taught an inner child workshop called Free the Heart and invited me to volunteer as a facilitator. I eagerly accepted. I had taken several similar workshops in Oakland and in Prescott, Arizona, and I loved the work. At that time, the inner child work was being offered to inmates in California and Nevada prisons. As it turned out, Sharie and her friend Kathleen were also volunteers. The three of us experienced an instant bond, quickly deepened by our work in the prisons and the accompanying road trips to and fro. We called ourselves the Three of Hearts and became sisters for life.

Inner child healing in a prison is deep work for all involved—volunteers and prisoners alike. We worked in "family circles" for two days, helping prisoners process the hurt of their families, early trauma, and a lifetime of misunderstanding, unresolved anger, shame, blame, and pain. Our work with men and women who had seemingly done the unforgivable was powerful beyond measure. We usually had fifty to sixty volunteers and 200 to 250 inmates participating at a time.

What I found most striking was seeing the changes in the demeanors and faces of the incarcerated as they were treated with kindness and respect through a two-day experiential educational program that included lectures, interactive and written exercises, and circle work. It seemed to open a place within of unexplored self-awareness—a new understanding of themselves and others that they could hold and accept more tenderly, if only for a few days at a time. The closing ceremony always brought every single person to tears. It included each male facilitator making an apology on behalf of all men. "If you have ever been mistreated . . . If you have ever been abused . . . If you have ever been disrespected . . . If you have ever been harmed . . . in any way . . . by a man . . . I apologize." Those words they offered personally and intentionally preceded passing out a single long-stemmed rose they had de-thorned by hand the night before. With a word of love—reflecting the intimacy of our work and the personal connection with each participant—women and men collapsed into the arms of facilitators and each other. It was extraordinary. Most of the tearful women I held in those ceremonies had never received a flower from a man, had never been treated kindly or with respect by a man, and certainly many of the Black women and Black men had never had a positive or trusting interaction with a white man or white woman at all. Ever.

I learned I could hold a loving space in the circle for a child molester. In our hotel room that night, Kathleen and Sharie held me as I tried to process the frightening enormity of that event.

Spiritual leaders have been known to blow up their creations and move on to their next expressions, and just as had happened with Mastery of the Heart School, our Oregon Free the Heart team eventually disbanded. But before that collapse of leadership occurred, we volunteered in prisons for about two years in total. The core principle of this level of circle work is to "do no harm." In retrospect, I'm not sure that we held up our side of the bargain. We were among a privileged group, with good intentions toward healing and belief in the work we were doing. But like many of those who work in the nonprofit and spiritual realms, our inexperience meant we couldn't begin to know the complexities of those we endeavored to serve. I can only hope that we did no harm in offering our utmost respect and love.

Sharie and Kathleen and I moved on, taking the gifts that exposure had given us, and road-tripped to the Oregon coast and to our favorite spot, Casa Rubio bed-and-breakfast in Smith River, California, when we wanted to get away. Kathleen died of breast cancer in 2014. She lives in our hearts and inspires me to imagine a world that works for everyone.

Love Sings

I always sang to the radio and records as a teenager and often when I was alone. I once believed I could sing, before my sister developed her voice as an opera singer with a befitting arrogance and a come-and-go pseudo-British accent that convinced me of her position as the one and only talented and necessary singer in the family.

I married a handsome R&B singer named Eddie with a soulful voice and a lot of charisma. I liked to listen and feel myself through his voice. Swoon-worthy, yes; no sing-along required.

I began voice lessons while living in Ashland, hoping that whatever was alive in my soul could exit my body through song. I met a woman about my age who worked with the same voice coach and had actually recorded a compact disc. I hoped my voice would express itself along the soulful lines of Janis Joplin and Aretha Franklin, but in accordance with my coaching notes, I practiced singing along with recordings of Norah Jones and CeCe Winans. Hardly second string!

Then I joined two choirs.

The Rogue River Valley Peace Choir was dedicated and thoughtful in song choice, arrangement, and intention. Dave, a caring man with a Beatles cover band that the town of Ashland danced to on Friday nights, directed the choir with spirit. In my second season with the choir, I auditioned—courageously but unsuccessfully—for a small group position but continued to flourish with the encouragement of my new teachers and friends. I could sing! My soprano range was clear and melodic and just needed strengthening. I was invited to try out again at the next opening.

Kathleen and Sharie joined the peace choir in my second year and we road-tripped once again for choir performances. A Seattle festival was a highlight. We sang in the car on the way up, all bought the same pair of soft, Chinese-embroidered Mary Janes at a street fair, then headed to a restaurant for dinner, got lost, and walked forever through what appeared to be a sketchy part of town. Another Three of Hearts adventure on the road of life and friendship.

The piano player for the peace choir directed the Threshold Choir, an organization created to offer the comfort of small singing groups attending the bedsides of people in care homes, hospices, and in palliative care. She led us in singing beautiful tonal harmonies to the old, the infirmed, and the dying, guiding them into the quiet, anchoring peace, and even ushering them into heaven. Imagining our notes opening that doorway gave me such peace and vocal ease.

But then my throat dried. I thought it might be the antidepressant I'd tried for a year, or maybe it was a loss of faith.

My notes grew shaky.

Tension built.

A desert erupted in my throat, and I lost my singing voice entirely.

I tried to find it. I tried to soothe it.

The moisture seeped out of my eyes and ran down my cheeks.

Then . . . silence.
Now I write
seeking a resonant word
to open a new chapter
with the choir of my heart and mind.

Spirit-Limited Love

For four years, my interior design company, Meridian Visions, was intermittently fruitful. When I was working in client homes—revitalizing them and making them beautiful—I couldn't have been happier! I loved encouraging people to live only with what they loved, helping them to release what actively drained their energy or simply no longer brought them joy. I loved rearranging things they had placed years before and not noticed since. I especially loved the big reveal: their surprise and joy after I had worked my magic.

I was following my bliss but living on savings. Funny that "follow your bliss and the money will come" just didn't pan out for me. I had done everything I understood I should do. What could my spiritual problem be? And that is where my spiritual convictions once again began to wobble as I questioned what part of "attracting abundance" I wasn't getting. The idea that if we do our part, meditate, pray affirmatively, make our list of desired qualities, align with the vortex, understand the laws of attraction, and keep our energy at the level of what we want to attract, everything should go our way and we should be happy—manifesting parking spots, princes, and a full pocketbook, right? Alas, still no happy ending and not enough money.

With the housing market collapse in 2008, Californians quit selling their houses and moving to Southern Oregon and the locals weren't spending money on redecorating their homes. The market price of my house turned upside down, leaving me owing more than the value of the house. I started packing, staged my house, and put it up for sale. Three months passed and I was about out of money. While I'd made invaluable friends and connections in Ashland, a feng shui consultant told me that my Ashland home was a "loser house with no support." I consulted Julian Lee, an astrocartographer—otherwise known as a relocation astrologist—and considered my next move.

Where Did You Say, Love?

Julian advised me to move "somewhere between Tampa and Naples on the gulf coast of Florida; you'll know when you get there." As instructed, I arrived in Tampa before sundown January 1, 2009. Within a day or two, I'd witnessed congestion, construction, confusion, frenetic energy, and only one pretty neighborhood. Tampa was not the place for me. I drove south. I took the coastal route, thinking I'd find the drive more scenic in my rented convertible— but, no. The drive was slow, hot, and boring, with no sign of water. *Florida—really?* Finally, I saw a BEACH sign and followed it right into St. Armands Circle in Sarasota. I wandered around the shops and down to Lido Beach, then wound back to choose a place for lunch. Chatting with the server, I remarked on how happy and nice everyone seemed to be, curious if that was the general mood. "Oh, yes," he said, "because it's always sunny. That makes us happy!" I returned to Tampa that night, checked out of my hotel the next morning, and drove back to Sarasota.

Restoring the Erotic

Dry like leaves and grass
Baked through summer.
Water runs over, downhill to lake and river
Absorbing none of the nutrients available.
You must run to ocean and dive deep
Where breath will be restored.
Surface slowly after swimming through kelp gardens
To meet self as mermaid, fish as friends.
Allow kelp to wrap body loosely.
Rest, breathe, float.
No rush.
Luxuriate.
Aloe will soften wrinkled skin,
Cloudy eyes will clear while peeking through bubbles at sun-
   beams.
Gentle movement lubricates joints and feelings long held firm.
Open, breathe.
Surface in a climax of joy, open to new life and luscious soften-
   ing of heart.

Love Considers Florida

On Sunday morning, I walked across the busy boulevard from Sarasota's Indigo Hotel into the flat-roofed symphony hall building doubling as a church that day. I struck up a conversation with the woman sitting next to me and discovered it was her first time there as well, although she lived locally on Longboat Key. Daphne and I made plans to meet for lunch the next day. She was leaving town a couple of days later for two weeks at a women's retreat center. I was interested in her plans and she in my adventures, so we found many things to talk about that afternoon over salads at Café Epicure. Our afternoon culminated in her offering a stay in her apartment while she was away.

Her apartment was gorgeous, obviously decorated by a professional in all-white, Florida style with birds of paradise and a private elevator that opened directly into the apartment foyer. Spacious floor-to-ceiling windows reached out to the water where the brown pelicans lived in nearby mangroves and a swimming pool surrounded by palm trees and lounges enticed me each day. *Heaven and free!* I felt blessed by Daphne's generosity and the magic raining down on me. Maybe abundance had finally decided to tumble in my direction.

Daphne's apartment was where I watched the January 2009 inauguration of Barack Obama as president of the United States of America. Alone, I let my emotions flow. I gave myself over to the beauty of the ceremonies and the presence and representation of all Black Americans, along with my belief that finally the leadership in America would move us toward a world that recognized the value and connection of all people. I saw that love in action truly is power: the promise of change built on a successful campaign of hope. This and so much more filled my heart to bursting.

Gratitude Love

Journal entry: January 21, 2009

"Happy" hardly describes my feelings today at seeing Barack Obama installed as our president. The love between Barack and his wife, Michelle, the voice of Aretha Franklin singing "My Country," and the power of this historical moment overwhelmed me as I watched the ceremonies and balls all day and all night. Thank you, God, for bringing this beautiful, brilliant, smart man and family to the face of America. He is a healer. He is articulate. He has depth and a soul he shares. I feel healed by his election. Our first Black president—who happens to be biracial. Knowing something about that part of his experience through my marriages, children, and life, I will hold him in the light of safety and empowerment.

Thank you, God, thank you. I am full of the magnificence of this two-day transition and grateful forever for all Barack Obama will bring to the world. No words could truly express what I feel and I guess I haven't wanted to try. I have just felt grateful to be alive and to witness the emotion, the healing, the gratitude, and the hope. Above all, the hope. It's a new day for the world, for the country, for me. There is opportunity here. I am open and so grateful to receive such blessings. For this and so much more, thank you. Thank you. Thank you. Reveal and provide my new home and work. Thank you and amen.

The very next day, I found my first Sarasota apartment on the corner of Morrill Street and Julia Place, surrounded by palms and across the street from the Towles Court art district. The apartment comprised the entire second floor of a funky, old, peach-colored house with aqua trim, located up a peeling, outdoor, wooden staircase that led to a yellow door with a purple glass doorknob. Turn the knob and enter into a small living room with knotty pine trim surrounding a little fireplace, unusable but charming. There, you will see beautiful, old pinewood floors, a large bedroom and a smaller, second room—bright with windows and sunlight—a small bathroom with a claw-foot tub and a tiny one-counter kitchen from hell. Oh, well. I didn't feel like cooking much anyway, but by the time I finished setting it up, I could cook when I got the notion. I was soon hosting gatherings and, yes, cooking once again as part of my joy in entertaining.

I painted the apartment in bright, Florida-lime green, yellow, and peach, and put it together like a jewel box. The building was featured on a local Segway tour and a couple of times each day, guides entertained tourists with stories of the building's colorful past as a brothel. For our first year in Sarasota, Codi and I made this eye-catching apartment our home.

My landlord allowed me to stay in the apartment without additional rent the last few nights I was in town before returning to Ashland to pack up. I bought a blowup mattress, a beach towel, and a set of sheets, and camped in my new apartment—getting a feel for it and arranging furniture in my mind. I met my neighbor Julie and her little Havanese pup. She generously loaned me some comfort items: A pillow. A lamp. Wineglasses. A beach chair. And her friendship. Each one offering small evidence of the goodness that seemed to surround me and encourage the adventure I was embarking on.

God's Love Explored

Journal entry: Monday, January 26, 2009

Back in Ashland, awake, as I often am at three in the morning.

As I wrote today's date, I remembered that it's been twenty-one years since GB died. Amazing. My journey, my story. A long time on my own. Now taking another huge step, moving to Florida out of the blue. I really will do anything! Here I am, living my yes, and reaching out to pray.

God, the Kingdom of Heaven, is my life. Given to me by God because I said yes, yes to life. Yes to this particular human experience. And now, yes to the vibration of my body, everything vibrating with the promise of new friends, a new home, and a return to a flow of money. Money coming to me in large amounts. That's part of the dream. What I am here to experience at this particular time.

I am open, with conviction, not knowing what is about to happen and saying yes anyway.

With some regularity, I debated with myself: questioned my faith and use of the word "God," the virtues of hope and positivity, and how to maintain my spirit. I would never return fully to the nothingness of my years as an atheist, but neither would I hold strong in the blended spirituality I had cobbled together. Wash! Rinse! Repeat!

But once again, I was resting in a belief of a higher power guiding and supporting me, loving me through this life. Surrounded by the magic and generosity unfolding during my move to Florida, I felt strengthened and supported by God, Goddess, the Universe, the Angels, Buddha, and all things spiritual and whole in nature. After all, Florida needed light beings. I felt brave, trusting my guidance to bring light wherever I was showing up.

Start with Loss

See the patterns and lose everything.
Lose your dad
Lose your mother
Lose your sister
Lose your innocence
Lose your faith.
Start over.

Lose your husband once
and then again
Lose friends
Feel the love in your heart die with each one.
Start over.

Lose your house
Lose sleep
Lose confidence
Lose your way, your timing, your zest for life.

Start over
with a swim in the ocean,
a walk in the powder-soft sand.
Watch what seemed lost return
in seashells and clouds.
No ribbons or bows this time.
No childhood dreams to be fulfilled,
just the sensation of breath.
Walk to a friend's.
Dance back home when you feel like it.
Wander down the road past memory lane.

Give generously then give something more.
Allow the space within to renew.
Let it empty again.
Let it fill.
Deep-breathe life back into your body.
Feel the anxiety return.
Try to remember love.
I didn't know survival would feel like this.

Love on the Road

Our beloved cat, Sylvia, had made the move to Ashland success-
fully, but I could tell she wasn't up for the trip to Florida. She
lived to be sixteen but crossed the Rainbow Bridge as I was considering next steps a few days before Christmas. I had planned a
Christmas Eve party, which turned out to be the only good reason
to get out of my robe and empty my tissue-filled pockets. On a

trip to Oakland, Bryan and I scattered Sylvia's ashes in Joaquin Miller Park in the Oakland Hills.

By March, Codi and I were ready for the road. We made the drive to Florida in ten days, visiting along the way. One night in Oakland with Bryan, one night in Los Angeles with Erin (my dear sistah-girlfriend, prayer partner, and the one person I always expect to have a happy ending), and two nights in Scottsdale with my childhood friend Marty. Memorable with Marty was a night out for dinner in a lovely outdoor cantina where a gentleman asked if he could buy our dogs a steak dinner—and he did. Next stop, Las Cruces, New Mexico, followed by Houston for one night with daughter of my heart, Heather, and her two sons. Next morning: on to New Orleans and her magic.

I love New Orleans, and this was my first visit after Hurricane Katrina. The devastation of Hurricane Katrina had stunned the world and the aftermath continued to wreak havoc and heartache. Again, the racial inequity in America was on full display. Codi and I walked the streets of the ninth ward and the French Quarter, taking pictures, collecting Mardi Gras beads, having coffee and beignets at Café Du Monde, and eating the best food ever. We would soon find ourselves pressed into service by the angels.

It happened while we were passing by an old church. Codi tugged on her leash in the direction of the wide, tall staircase leading up to the church's massive wooden doors and entryway. *Show me the way, Codi.* As we neared the top, I noticed a woman sitting on the steps, crying, her face to her knees and her broken heart pouring out around her, almost visibly. She looked up as we approached. Codi and I spent the next two hours sitting on those steps beside her. The depth of her sorrow was great and her plan was suicide. After we'd spoken with this woman and listened to her story, she appeared to be in a different frame of mind. I believe Codi and I were guided by angels as instruments of love to help change her mind. The experience seemed magical.

I've considered escape by death during depressive and hopeless times throughout my life. The journey through the desperation of living—wishing to be free of it—marks a monumental effort. I have dived deep into emotional and spiritual exploration and, at my lowest times, sat at my table anticipating how little the knife through my brain could possibly hurt. I have never gone to a set of church steps to say my final goodbyes to God as our woman did. I have gutted my way through the hours and days of that level of despair. Fascinated by the will to live when working with cancer patients, I had often wondered how that bit of humanness had bypassed me. Two things have kept me here: One, I could not leave Holly and Bryan on purpose, even after they became adults, and two, I came to understand that death by suicide would not give me the outcome I really wanted. The thing I have been after all my life. I want to love my life. I had to get to a place within myself where I valued my life—the one that included death and depression, disappointment, and change. But also: courage, love, success, and intention.

Sitting with our woman, Codi's head in her lap, I spoke what my heart was guided to say. I think the angels were with us—as I believe they have been with me in my times of need—helping me to "choose love" and find a way through the darkness. In our time on the stairs, we helped our woman move through her dark moment and choose another path.

A healing peace filled all three of us as we said our goodbyes. Codi and I extended our stay another night and soaked in the mystery of our time on the steps and the magic of New Orleans swirling around us. Following an unremarkable one-night stay in Tallahassee, we pulled into our new home in Sarasota.

Codi was a great travel companion and would live another three years with me in Sarasota. Best dog ever, she crossed the Rainbow Bridge at eighteen, having helped me to make many friends. Together, we explored neighborhoods, states, mountains, beaches—and church steps.

Love Opens Doors

I had driven all the way across the country without any idea of what I would do when I got to Sarasota, boldly trusting my intuition and believing Spirit would continue supporting this adventure and lead me to work. I filled my days walking around town, visiting design firms, décor shops, hospitals, and medical buildings. An experienced networker, I joined the Greater Sarasota Coaches Alliance, where I met two lifelong friends: Elena, initially thanks to our mutual appreciation of the poet David Whyte, followed by her intellectual brilliance and ability to create an itinerary well beyond the average imagination, and Gail, goddess extraordinaire, author, archetype coach, Nia trainer, and all-around creative inspiration. I met George while out walking Codi. George, who knew no strangers, invited me to dinner. Through George and his husband, David, I met many others, and through each one of these meetings, my circle expanded. I met people at a creativity fair, first Friday festivals, restaurants, on boats while walking in the marina, and, through joining singles' groups. Soon, I was boating, dancing, walking, going to the beach, the Ringling Museum of Art and Ca' d'Zan, Selby Botanical Gardens, and taking part in my first writing group. Making new friends had never been a problem and I had learned to be comfortable venturing out on my own.

As I was composing a letter to send with my resume to local doctors, I interviewed for a part-time, marketing/medical billing job with a primary care group. On my way to hop on a boat for a day with friends, I got the call, offering me the job. A champagne celebration on board fulfilled the day.

I didn't last two weeks in what I thought would be a low-key, easy-breezy position that allowed time for other creative pursuits. This practice needed help with a capital "H." I wrote a proposal for a practice administrator position and left a copy on the partners' desks. Pat Contino, MD, raced out of his office with a big smile, waving the letter and emphatically nodding, "Yes!"

For the next five years, I had my hands full with multiple re-organizations, relocations, provider changes, H1N1 flu, the sale of the practice to a hospital system, and its reclamation and conversion to concierge medicine. I gave it my all and got back into health care full swing. But by the time I left my Florida practice, I had once again lost my excitement and all hope for health care's evolution.

Forgiveness-Work as a Path

Be thankful for what disturbs and forgive it.
Forgive myself for being tired,
For many days wanting to do something other than my job.
Forgive that I wish I didn't have to work.
For wanting a large sum of money to magically appear in my life
    and free me!
Forgive me for wanting to feel some appreciation and respect.

For wanting to be free of problem-focused health care
and its overall driver and creative limitation: money.
The mirror—my work
The answer—forgive
The moment—I'm tired
The answer—forgive
Mastery books on my lap,
I seek a sense of worthiness,
and find only the drain I'm circling.
A few more days of "Why bother?" narrow to "Why?"
and the weariness of "What's the point?"
Judging, forgiving, judging, forgiving.
Years of journals documenting self-judgment,
feasting and fasting, opening and closing, dissatisfaction,
until finally, no satisfaction.
Depression hovers.
Work so entrenched in waste—I want to run,
if only I had the courage or the energy.
What's the point?
Forgive me.
This is burnout, not reality.
In reality, it's 3:00 a.m. and I need sleep.
Get up.
Go to work.
Why?
Why not?
Don't want to.
Need money.
No fun.
No meaning.
No connection.

Keep moving the pieces.
No impact,
No progress,
No peace.
Will you live a wasted life?
Not possible.
Then why does it feel pointless, loveless, lacking?
Never falter,
Hardly sleep,
Love is lost,
Why I weep.
Held too tight in life's restraint,
Praying to yet another saint.
Broken heart and rage within,
Find sudden rapture in the wind,
As gentle breezes wander through,
A yellow boat on sea of blue.
Lazy daze,
Blank on white.
Color walls,
Paint them bright.
Paint again as perspectives change.
Paint them soft, allow the range
Of true expression calling me,
Calling all of life to be free.
Yet here I am and here I'll stay
wasting yet another day
in the insane system in which I work.
This is burnout, not reality.
Disconnected and alone,
with the wind chime to remind me

there is more than my fatigued thoughts,
more than this void I keep trying to fill.
This is a dried-up, uncomfortable life just now.

In graduate school in 1981, I did an internship at the Haight-Ashbury's Women's Needs Center for their free medical clinic and later became a board member. The clinic motto was "Health care for people, not for profit." I have long awaited universal health care in our country and strongly support the declaration: "Health care is a right, not a privilege." I embrace that commitment to humanity and believe it to be essential to the support of human civility, connection, and community. And yet my livelihood has been based in the for-profit system, and part of my job has been to ensure a healthy bottom line.

In some ways, my work has been a distraction from grief, giving me focus and purpose. Like many people, I have worked to make money to afford a good life for my children and a life that I could enjoy too. I achieved that. Apart from my kids, work is what I have thought about most of the time. I have often made work a priority to the exclusion of my own needs, desires, and self-care. When packing for a vacation to Paris or a weekend away, I rarely knew what was in the suitcase or anything about my destination. I could, however, tell you every detail about the projects I had completed in the weeks before getting to the airport and often found myself engaging in last-minute calls while boarding a plane or even during the first few days of a trip. Amid the life I cultivated, my paycheck became the Prince and I was still

Cinderella, working hard to stay ahead of the deep sorrow within and the depression that lingered around me.

Health care is not an easy career choice. Most people go into medicine for good and humanitarian reasons, but something happens along the way to change that. We learn that health care is focused on problems and symptoms and the absence of health—health often not restored for boundless reasons. We learn that not everyone is equal in the health care system, a system too often driven by money rather than values. We also learn that what is required of those who work in health care is not healthy at all; it is demanding, the hours are long, and the quality of the results are not guaranteed. Good people with good intentions lose their vision and communication within the system often lacks compassion or pragmatic guidance.

But I'm a problem-solver, a change facilitator. I was dedicated and I enjoyed the professional world. I persevered. What eventually diminished and ultimately destroyed my satisfaction in "working hard" for the health care system was when my work began to lack meaning and connection either to the people in the system, the culture of that system, or those who were being served by it. This feeling is a lonely and thankless one, also known as burnout.

On the flip side, over the course of my career, my work as a medical practice administrator, coach, and consultant has supported physicians in empowered decision-making, business development, and leadership. I drove these physicians toward success in the most creative, compassionate ways I could conceive of—all geared toward vastly improving their self-awareness and personal fulfillment. I clarified options, compiled data, built budgets, and guided healthy discussions, and I focused on creating healthy organizations and satisfying, expansive work environments and business models. This is the part of my working life that I loved.

I am grateful for the wake of goodwill and appreciation that trails behind me. I value the relationships as much, probably more, than the goals I accomplished. I only worked with doctors I felt were the best in their field. Nothing I could do for them could make them better clinicians, but I was fully prepared to help them be successful business owners and maybe even better people while they were at it.

I had learned through my many years of working in the medical field that the assumed, if not inherent, power that comes with the role of physician causes some of them to lose their sense of self as healers and community members, undermining their interactions with patients and staff. I believe all physicians should be inspired—if not mandated—to develop a degree of self-awareness and be trained in compassionate speech and active listening before interacting with patients and managing employees. Rarely do physicians enjoy the business and management side of their practices, and as a result, few develop any skill in that area. And of course, doctors commonly experience burnout. With that observation in mind, I started consulting and coaching physicians and health care providers and ultimately created a business called Practice With CARE. (I purposefully capitalized the word "CARE" to stand for the following: "C," Create a culture of commitment and caring; "A," Activate your assets and life vision; "R," Redesign your practice to include core strategies and value alignment, and; "E," Evolve personally and professionally to make your experience and effort count.)

In my ongoing desire to have meaningful work and contribute to the well-being of others, I also created Women 'Round the Table. This became a seven-week group series designed to expand the creativity and courage of participants toward living lives they loved. As the saying goes, "we teach what we need to learn." In each series, I led groups of women through a curriculum I wrote and titled, Getting from Here to There. The title came from what I had noticed while leading a staff meeting one day in Florida: the difference in where we are—here—and where we want to go— there—was the letter "T." I asked myself what the "T" was. "Time!" It takes *time* to get from here to there. What is time and how best can we use it? (T for "Tools for transformation," I for "Intention/implementation/inspiration," M for "Mentoring/ meaning/milestones," and E for "Energy and excellence.")

Engaging with my creative spirit brings me joy. By sharing the tools and experience I have gained on the path of learning to love my life, I supported the women at my table and doing so gave me a deeper sense of purpose. I loved watching groups and individuals transform.

Many Teachers, Many Paths
My Unpublished Résumé from A to Z

Position: Mother, seeker, teacher, healer, coach

Purpose: Connect, learn, love

Method: Experience, study, share, imagine

A: Academy of self-knowledge, ayahuasca, angels, acupuncture, astrology, astrocartography, archetypes, Ayurvedic medicine, Abraham teachings, attachment theory, acceptance, affirmations

B: (The) Breaking Free program, breath work, Buddhism, behavior therapy, bachelor's degree in holistic health, being alone, business coaches, board membership (Women's Needs

Center, Northern California Medical Group Management Association, Easter Seals of Sarasota)

C: Callings, critique, craniosacral therapy, color consulting, creative communication, collage, committed living, ceremony, cancer counseling, Chinese Medicine, coaching, chiropractic care, chamber of commerce memberships and leadership programs

D: Dream art and interpretation, design, redesign and staging, death and dying workshops and hands-on care, drumming, depression

E: Eye-movement desensitization and reprogramming (EMDR), enneagram, Esalen retreats and workshops

F: Family systems therapy, family constellation work, Freeing a Woman's Heart to Love and Free the Heart workshops, feminine wisdom, floating, feng shui, friendships

G: Goddesses, gratitude and grace, getting from here to there, group process training

H: Healing your inner child, hypnotherapy, homeopathy, holistic health, human design, Heller work

I: Intuition development, integrative medicine, ice plunging

J: Journaling

K: Kinesiology, Kentro Body Balance

L: Leadership, Louise Hay's life interpretation guidance, love, LSD, living through the heart

M: Meditation, Mastery of the Heart School, medical group management, massage, mushrooms, master's degree in health services administration, Meridian Visions, marriage

N: Namaste training, neurolinguistic programing (NLP), Nonviolent Communication training, new thought spirituality, numerology, network spinal analysis

O: Organizational development, oneness

P: Peace choir, psychic reading, pilates, prayer and prisons, poetry, Practice With CARE

Q: Quiet time alone

R: Reiki, reading, Rolfing

S: Systems theory, Science of Mind, shiatsu, the seven habits of highly effective people, somatic therapy, somatic writing, sacred travel, sweat lodges, sound baths, singing crystal bowls, Saboteur-Muse Project, Soul Collage, Season for Nonviolence, Stephen Levine, swimming with dolphins in the wild

T: Threshold Choir, 1:1 therapy and groups crying in the woods on weekends, tarot, three of hearts, tai chi, Thai massage, travel: the Bimini islands of the Bahamas, the cities of Hong Kong and Paris, the countries of Brazil, Canada, Japan, Mexico, South Africa, Taiwan, and twenty-seven US states, including one district (Arizona, California, Colorado, Florida, Georgia, Hawaii, Illinois, Louisiana, Maine, Maryland, Massachusetts, Mississippi, Nevada, New Jersey, New Mexico, New York, North Carolina, Oregon, Rhode Island, South Carolina, Tennessee, Texas, Utah, Washington, Washington, DC, Vermont, and Wyoming)

U: Unraveling the past, uncomfortable (states of being)

V: Visioning, vision boards, volunteering

W: Weed, writing, walking, Watsu, Women 'Round the Table, wild writing, willingness

X: X-static dancing

Y: Yoga

Z: Zip-lining, zigzagging through life while learning to loosen my grip

I am a student of life: one of those lifelong learners who can't keep from buying the next book or enrolling in the next class sparking my attention. I am fascinated by the creativity of others and what inspires them to create. As one who thought she was not creative, I began my recovery by affirming "I am a creative being" as I walked up and down the hills in my Oakland neighborhood early in the morning before work. I kept up the repetition and began to see a change in my belief. In the realm of creativity, I kept reading, studying, learning more, and meeting new people.

I have not included the many authors, musicians, keynote speakers, or folks on the path whose brilliance made an impression or all of the professional, spiritual, and educational seminars and programs I have taken, simply because I can't even remember them all, and along with those burned journals mentioned at the beginning, I've recycled boxes and boxes of binders and notebooks from classes, programs, and projects. Moving across the country a couple of times is a motivator for getting rid of a lot of stuff on so many levels.

I value work in personal growth, meditation, and spiritual inquiry, and feel these practices have improved the quality of my life. Through my work and study, I have sought and developed awareness of my reason for being and my connection to source energy and all that is and improved my self-care habits and body image. I courageously persevere when life is hard. I do my best to stay aligned with my values and I strive to be a better person on this earth. I have not narrowed my understanding to a moment of transcendence, a belief in any possibility of my enlightenment, or even a single, sustainable belief system, but I am able to hold the dark and the light with some measure of humility, understanding that life is always changing and as humans we are here to grow. And, with all my tools and training, I have repeatedly become depleted and depressed and pretended to be happier than I actually feel. I also hibernate when that's the best I can do.

Love Calls Home

After five years in Florida, I felt complete. I had made wonderful friends and acquired an active social life. I loved living near the beach and swimming, boating, and fishing in the Gulf of Mexico. Yet, something was nudging me, calling me into the unknown once again. I was thinking of writing more and expanding my consulting. In my search for more joy, I resigned from my job. Now I needed to recreate my revenue stream.

I visited Holly in Atlanta, imagining travel would be part of my consultancy and thinking I'd need a more accessible airport. I loved the areas off the Beltline in Atlanta. Holly and I walked around, looking at options—Atlanta being a possibility for sure— until I heard "Go home!" The inner voice I trusted was speaking to me again. The voice that speaks lovingly and reminds me to "choose love" was calling me home. I knew that meant returning to California. I talked it over with Bryan and he welcomed the idea.

As was the case with each of my moves, friends, family, and the universe supported me on this new path. I put the belongings that made the cut into storage and gave away or sold everything else. I shipped my car and Holly flew home with me, helping to carry my two cats, Groove and Davis. We arrived in Oakland on October 6, 2014, the night before my sixty-sixth birthday. We had a wonderful celebration dinner at Burma Superstar—a popular Burmese restaurant in the Bay Area—as I absorbed the vibrant and diverse energy of Oakland. The cats and I stayed with Bryan, grateful for his welcome and generosity. By Thanksgiving, I had secured an apartment for December. Then, in December, a primary care practice offered me a practice

186 · MERIDIAN KRISTI

administrator position. I spent January getting settled and deco-rating, then started my new job in February 2015. The divine support I sometimes receive amazes me.

I spent the next six years developing the management of my new practice and helping to create a future vision and a culture of caring. My new position had its challenges, but that was the nature of the job. I thrived for a few years, thinking I'd found a great place to land for my final hurrah in health care. I felt blessed by the open hearts of the founding partners, and as we brought in new providers, I nurtured a foundation of mentoring, respect, and trust that we continued to strengthen. A year into my tenure, we made a strategic decision to affiliate our primary care group with a larger, multispecialty organization. After working another three to four years, I was beginning to feel that I had stretched the prac-tice as far as my doctors were comfortable with for the time being, leaving me to question if I was replete with what I had to offer.

As has happened with every job I've assumed in health care administration, I reached a place where I could either develop new projects, move on, or suffer an extended period of discon-nection until something shifted. I worked with a therapist and then a coach to see the good in my work and to sort out why I often felt like part of the furniture, why I felt alone in my efforts. I was back into the cycle of endings and beginnings. At the end, but not done! Wash! Rinse! Wrung out!

ACT VII

Love for a Country

In 2016, a blatant misogynist, narcissist, racist, and all-around hateful man was elected president of the United States. As healing as I'd found the election of Barack Obama, the election of Donald Trump was devastating and inconceivable. Two days after Trump was elected, I was leaving a meeting at work when one of the pro-Trump doctors said he was "sorry the election was so hard for me." Tears welled up as I turned toward him and spoke. "Everything I value is at stake now."

On March 11, 2020, near the start of the pandemic, that same doctor compassionately encouraged me to "please go home before it's too late." We really had no idea what we were facing, but I was the oldest person in the practice and age was one COVID-19 risk factor we already understood. Nine days later, on March 20, California mandated that all citizens shelter in place.

COVID brought to light the thinly veiled inequities of our health care system. Trump opened the gates of hell. These were the times we were living in. I was reminded that this was an unpredictable life. I grieved the loss and the lost. I mourned the violence and hatred. I reached beyond my outrage toward love and prayed for a kinder world, making room in my heart for such hope. It was not enough.

188 · MERIDIAN KRISTI

On May 19, day sixty-nine of my shelter-in-place, work-at-home life, I learned that one of the managers I had been mentoring for a few years had resigned. No call, no communication—apparently no trust or respect, either. The manager simply emailed two weeks' notice to one of the doctors. Upset and home alone, I tried replacing my anger and sense of being betrayed and disrespected by calling the manager to talk over her decision and approach. I met with only partial success. The manager did have a change of mind and stayed, but as time would reveal, she never told me her truth and it hurt me.

Writing about work events helped me process the tough times. I've learned that through writing, we can clarify our individual understanding of challenges and I believed that during the pandemic, what was learned and written would become part of our survival story. Survivors of COVID-19 would also become the creators of all that was new and hopefully more beautiful, loving, healthy, inclusive, thoughtful, and kind.

And then . . .

1. On the evening of May 25, 2020, a white cop in Minneapolis killed a Black man named George Floyd by kneeling on his neck while two other cops restrained him and a third prevented the gathering crowd from intervening. This time, people all over the country were sitting at home watching the replays of him dying on television, over and over and over again—all nine minutes and twenty-nine seconds of his brutal, horrifying murder. Armored as we are by violence as entertainment, even America found it hard to watch.

2. No longer able to ride out shelter-in-place in the numbing comfort of our homes (depending on your circumstances, political affiliation, or frame of mind), people went to the streets in massive numbers to call attention to Floyd's murder. This time, white America could not sidestep the outrage or claim ignorance about this familiar and frequently repeated story of police brutality, racism, and racial injustice in America.

3. Protests against racism and police brutality against African Americans became the focus, and COVID-19 masks were worn around the necks of protesters, more as acknowledgement of the pandemic than as protection from it. Voices needed to be heard, not muffled.

4. Maybe this time we would open to a deeper truth and healing. Maybe this time real change was in our future. And maybe this time the best and the worst of us would meld together in plain sight and manifest the truth of our connection and the absolute mandate to love. Maybe this time we would choose an inclusive and better life for every living being—no exceptions. We were late, but maybe this time.

5. I picked a Facebook "fight" with an old friend over a racially misinformed and offensive post. She was one of three Republican friends I knowingly still spoke to thinking I knew her loving heart. In her defense, she sent me a link and asked me to listen to her Sunday church service. I didn't.

6. I worked with some Republicans. I carried on with my work like I couldn't see their politics and they didn't see mine. My diplomacy might have made things easier for them but it certainly did little to ease my disgust.

7. My neighbor Mary died unexpectedly on a Friday night. Not of COVID.

8. I missed my friends, but I didn't.

9. I was lonely, but I wasn't.
10. I wanted to go out, but I felt safer at home.
11. I didn't know what it meant to feel safe anymore; it might have been one of the last illusions I held on to. I watched the threads of illusion unravel.
12. As my outrage expanded, I was uncomfortable with this magnitude of uncertainty.
13. Still, I held on, because Black Lives Matter, and because maybe this time we would choose an inclusive, equitable, and better life for every living being.

I heard someone in a Zoom class say that "being yourself can be a revolutionary act." Yes. I'm living it now: being myself and taking the hits as they come while still seeking a peaceful, intelligent, creative path and opportunities to make a meaningful contribution to the effort. With all of my life skills and determination intact, I am not at all sure that I have what it will take to rise above the heartache and violence of today's politics in America. I want to, but I wonder how as I write from the remaining chapter of my life—not yet complete but of unknown duration. Always true but more immediate now. As I continue to address hard truths, I do it with wavering confidence but a committed and sustained desire to leave a better, more loving world for our children.

Love Carries On

I continued working from home. I tried to give the managers my forty-five years of education, insight, and experience via Zoom. Trump was still president. Under his reign and via his encouragement, Americans and others continued to normalize racism and inexcusable, hateful behavior. COVID still raged and developing information about the pandemic was inconsistent and therefore unreliable. Mass shootings and gun violence devastated more communities. Police continued to kill Black men and women. I got my work done, but no matter where I perched with my computer, the world I saw through my window was a mess.

War is Threatening. Will it be Civil or Universal?

Relentless in my desire to open my heart and love my life,
I unfold where the union of love and loss are laid out like a
    picnic blanket.
I open the imaginary basket to see what is revealed.
What rare foods can I blend to create something sweet and
    savory?
Something warm and delicious. But the chardonnay of the even-
    ing blends with my brain and moves my pen in circular
    thoughts of uncertainty, reflecting the days we are living.
Melodic symbols of past bliss play to the uncertain future of po-
    litical insanity and prayers for the security of my beloveds.
A virus has threatened health and well-being. I reconsider most
    every plan.
Time passes. I question how much or how little is available and
    wonder how I will measure its value. Considering how I
    spend my time, what I think about, what I do, leads to re-
    viewing the past and a hesitant peek into the future where all
    is unknown. I ponder the mysteries: the coronavirus and why
    its impact is so personal, so vast, so frightening. And
    Trump's legacy: so personal, so vast, so frightening.

I spend time reviewing the daily CDC (Centers for Disease Control and Prevention) updates, summarizing information into COVID-19 practice protocols and trying to offer accurate information to providers previously accustomed to feeling confident about helping patients and returning them to health as quickly as possible. But not now. Now we are all in the dark, with only one fool—the head of our nation—who claims to know. He tells us to inject bleach and looks over at his shocked experts for confirmation. In stunned silence, outrage blooms. Will anyone brave his ire and let the impetuous emperor know he has again shown his naked stupidity?

Fear has reached a new level. Surprising—as I have so often thought that things couldn't get worse—but today, this crazy man speaks another lie. Those who count transgressions say he has lied over seventeen thousand times in the past three years of his presidency. The cost of lying magnifies for me.

I need refuge. I search through the haze of my confusion and lost hope. I need to find my inner strength, my interior wisdom. I list a few things I can contribute to the tipping point needed to counter the injustice and pain of each day: a way of being, a few things to appreciate about myself in the darkness, a few things that might encourage love in the light of day. It's a short list in the face of all that needs to be outweighed, but here goes . . . I need to make this list because it's coronavirus time and many people will die unexpectedly. Maybe I will be one of them.

Contributions to love's tipping point:

1. I try hard to understand.
2. I make spaces beautiful.
3. I can be fearless and sometimes terrified in equal measure.

4. I have proven to be resilient.

5. I try to learn from my mistakes.

6. I'm willing to reconsider.

7. I'm a good listener.

8. Sometimes, I channel really good information.

9. I love taking care of things and decorating space and body.

10. I'm scared of bees and appreciate feeling like someone will protect me.

11. I was once a good cook, but I'm seriously out of practice. With a lover to encourage me, I might improve.

12. I wear sunglasses most of the time. But behind them, my eyes are glistening.

13. I like to read and get lost in the brilliance of elegant words and a flowing story.

14. I know how to be quiet and together without needing constant conversation.

15. I like to bring out the best in others.

16. When I'm angry, I like to talk through my anger and work it out.

17. Sometimes, talking about my anger scares me; sometimes, it scares other people.

18. I am able and willing to feel my feelings and to share them.

19. I like deep and personal conversations.

20. I like to feel adored and cared for.

21. I know how to make a sincere apology and will accept the same.

22. I'm curious and I like to learn about what others think.

23. I am a practicing writer.

24. I am getting braver about sharing my writing.

25. I love when a poem emerges, when all of a sudden it's there on the page.
26. I want to be seen as my authentic self. I abhor insincerity.
27. Sometimes I feel lonesome.
28. I am a good friend, but it's become harder to be one during COVID and political divergence.
29. I love to go to the beach.

The shift from depression to love can happen in an instant or over the course of a lifetime. It can happen again and again. I keep choosing to remember the good about me, choosing to love and do what moves me in the direction of that goodness as best as I can. Doing so is a choice and my commitment to loving my life. Doing so also requires that I call bullshit now and then.

This Poem

This poem cannot wind your alarm clock
but it can tell you it's time to wake up.
It can tell you that I care that you wake up,
that it is important that you wake up.
It might give you insight or lead you down a garden path, in-
    spired,
choosing not to return, because the light is so bright, so beautiful.
This poem might address a need,
introduce you to a thought or make you laugh.
It made me cry as it poured onto the page.
It made me wonder at the resolve it takes to live.
It made me speak in tongues unfamiliar
and dance down deep into the horror of the times.

This poem may not seem like a poem to you.
Call me selfish, but I will write it still
Because it is an invitation.
This poem will not change you unless you accept its invitation.
The invitation that comes from my desire to meet your heart
    and feel it open.
This poem may show you that you are still you,
And I am still me, and we are here together.
We are inextricably here together to experience this time of
    COVID-19
and determine what is necessary now, together.
It speaks to our humanity and calls attention to those
who have been overlooked and under-cared for,
by design.
This poem may not speak to you or open your heart,
But if it doesn't,
Goddamn it—you need to wake up! The alarm already sounded.

In Service to Love's Drifting

Politics and COVID brought new friends to my living room.
They are smart and stand up for what I care about in this time
    of political and racial reckoning.
No pesky opinions to disagree with are likely to intrude.
They require none of my cooking or entertaining skills, and I eat
    and drink with them daily.
Thanks, MSNBC.
My real-life friends, those who do best with some human atten-
    tion, also live in the small screen boxes on their computers.

We Zoom or talk on the phone. We eat in each other's ears, and
   sometimes, we disagree.

Now I Lay Me Down to Sleep

Helicopters circling overhead. I take a sip of cool water: my last
   for the night, I hope.
With drowsy eyes and ponytailed hair, I lay my book down.
I roll to the left and pull my knees up. Pillows tucked up just
   right, I lightly press the sheet over my exposed ear and gently
   begin to pray for my brown-skinned children. I hear my internal, eternally whispered longing for safety and peace,
   justice, health, and love for all. I begin to drift, no longer
   aware of the words or conscious thought.
Without warning, my body betrays me. My stomach roils, my
   legs jump, my body goes hot, and my feet go cold. I am alert.
I've missed the moment.
That luxurious moment on the other side of relaxation.
The moment when I drop off and cross the bridge of prayer to
   peace.
I so long for sleep.
I shift. I listen. I fan my face and put socks on my feet.
I turn on the light. I begin again.
Book in hand, I will ease toward prayer, hoping this time my
   body will find peace and go deeper, releasing the despair of
   the day, the weeks, the months, this lifetime.
My bed is a refuge from the world outside. A place where the
   stars align, my dreams go silent, and the sound of helicopters
   becomes a softer backdrop than an hour ago.

Despite a million prayers and busy angels, there will be no peace
    in America tonight
and I have little hope for tomorrow.
Sleep, rest this body
worn fragile by despair for yet another Black man
killed at the hands of a white cop tonight.
And the cities burn with passion.

And So Love Goes . . . COVID in Fall 2020
September 8, 2020

After the 446th mass shooting this year in the United States of
America—five injured in Baltimore, Maryland, including a
seventeen-year-old, when a gunman opened fire on a group of
people playing dice—it's hard to know what to say. I set the alarm
for time to write before I begin another at-home workday but hit
the snooze button twice.

    I took a pound of ground turkey from the freezer and won-
dered what I might make for dinner. I considered looking for
recipes online, then remembered Bryan would bring dinner, because it's Tuesday and my son brings dinner over on Tuesdays. I
put the turkey back in the freezer.

    I make tea. I've been out of coffee for a few days. I'm not sure
I care. It hasn't tasted good lately.

    After the 446th mass shooting, the fires rage in the cities and
the mountains. Why would you take fire to the woods in August
to celebrate the gender of your unborn child and through your
negligence ruin your lives and the lives of so many others? The
fires are not yet contained; the smoke covers the clouds and drips
down over my COVID-19 mask. It follows me into the house

and fills my rooms with a sad, familiar smell. It's fire season in California and it came early this year. That we now have a season called "fire" screams more evidence of the stupidity and carelessness on this planet.

On a day like this, after the 446th mass shooting, I have turned on my computer to get on a Zoom meeting, but in the face of rampant violence and fire, nothing seems of real importance. Our agenda matters to those whom we still employ during the pandemic and those who will be affected by what we decide today. It matters to the patients we care for. But in the scheme of things, I wonder. I'm so unhappy about every little thing. But today, the big things are monstrously overwhelming. Why don't we talk about what matters first, then turn toward work? I think I have too many things tangled together in this season in which I have lost all hope.

The train is still running through downtown. I still love that faraway sound and the gentle memories it initiates. Nearer are the garbage trucks banging around outside, bringing me back to present moment realities. My friend Grace is dying while I fall silent but never stop thinking about her. I miss the days of our past while staying present to her needs.

After the 446th mass shooting, the birds are still flying, the squirrels leap through the branches of nearby old oak trees and flatten on my patio in the hundred-degree weather, tongues hanging, their little chests pounding. The plants are alive in their pots, and I sit still and think about watering them.

September 10, 2020

On my way out the door to care for Grace today, the healing crystal Kathleen had brought me from Brazil spoke to me. "Take me with you to Grace!" it said, and I did. It brought her comfort as she held it and moved it over her body all afternoon.

We talked, Grace and I. "Do you know how much longer you want to stay, my friend?"

"Not long," she said. "I am at peace. My heart too." And after a few minutes of silence, "I love you, Meridian. I am so glad you're with me."

"Me too, Grace. I'm glad I'm with you too."

Later, she whispers, "The spirit of God is within me."

"Yes," I say, and I believe her, though I've never heard her say such a thing in over forty years of friendship. But I know it's true and we are together in Spirit now as we always have been.

I've set my coffee somewhere. My throat feels dry; is it sore? God, don't let it be COVID.

The hospice nurse came. She said Grace could linger for weeks, in which case we would need more help to keep up her twenty-four-hour care. I couldn't imagine how that could be possible, though. This would be Grace's timing. Meanwhile, Grace and I talked about eternal joy and sweet memories, much more reassuring to me.

Grace, Beth, and I had walked into the hot tubs in San Francisco in the '80s carrying our bags, our water, our pot, and a full-length mirror. We were bold. We were curious. We were seeking a more expansive understanding and acceptance of our feminine bodies, our shapes and weight. Three women uniquely connected and becoming more of who we were, because for over twenty-five years, we met weekly with commitment and love. Together, we deepened, asked questions, helped each other to recognize our patterns, and shared truth from our hearts. We each had many friends and we were well loved. We introduced our friends and colleagues, had amazing parties and meaningful experiences, but our threesome was special and we held it sacred. We supported each other across the expanse of life: husbands, births, deaths, kids, careers, choices, food, drug experimentation, education and teaching, celebrations and sorrows.

Eighteen years have passed since Beth died of cancer. I sense she will come for Grace anytime now. Let go, my dear friend. You are complete. You've given it all. Be free! I love you.

September 13, 2020

I feel dull inside, absent without understanding of something so fundamental as the will to live.

For the life of me, I don't understand. When the process of dying is all there is to look forward to, does one more hug or one more smile make a difference? I suppose it could if it was the very one you needed before goodbye. But who is Grace waiting for? Or what is she waiting for? Our team of caregiving friends consider the upcoming election her most likely reason for waiting. She definitely wants Trump voted off the planet. The singing crystal bowls were playing softly in the background today, when out of the quiet space we were holding for her, Grace said, "I'm tired of those bowls. Turn on MSNBC!" We cracked up and, as we waited, allowed laughter to ease the urgency of our bodies.

How can I wish away anything she still wants? For me, I want to be so current that nothing remains for me to wait for and all I have received is enough. But I won't know how I'll feel for sure until it is my time. I trust Holly and Bryan will always know that I love them, and I know that they will miss me. But I never want to stretch out the end—it's awful, at least for those sitting bedside, tending and waiting. At least it is for me. But here I am again, this time at Grace's bedside, and I wouldn't be anyplace else.

The air: gray and heavy with ash, the only remains of trees and homes, memories, animals, beloveds and belongings, all that was so recently alive now soot floating hundreds of miles to be breathed in by what is left of humanity and become part of my cells, my memories, our collective sorrow and grief. It's fire season.

Your home lives in my lungs, and in the words of Eric Garner, the forty-three-year-old African American who repeated seventeen times while dying in a police chokehold in Staten Island, New York: "I can't breathe." His words created a wave of cultural revolution and continue to reverberate in my body. Tears have washed the smile from my eyes while my clenched jaw twitches with a lost thought, words that can't escape between my teeth or my narrowed throat. Or slip around the edges of my COVID mask.

Will there be joy again? How about blue skies and fresh air? The loss grows heavier, more expansive, and I can't understand how this has become our life.

September 16, 2020

I didn't think I could be this angry and this sad at the same time in one disconnected body. The convergence is explosive, but lethargy allows it to just keep circulating through my veins, my muscles gone flabby, my bones dangling with no purpose, no intention.

I didn't think it was possible for the climate to burn up the earth in my lifetime, even though I've known our destructive, uncaring nature would catch up to us one day. "One day" is here now, and still I can't imagine one more hurtful thing happening, and then another catastrophe awakens.

I didn't think:
I could feel this numb,
I would have so little energy,
Grace would last this long,
I would be so exhausted by it,
I could be so callous as to wish her life away, but I do
And I feel bad about it.
I will take the internet seminar on happiness and hope to learn
    how to manage myself better.

September 17, 2020

6:16 p.m., Grace is gone.
She made an impact
blessing and healing many with her love and medicine.
Grace was a healer, a nurse, a comforter, a skilled clinical expert,
    an educator, a mother,
And my dear friend.

September 19, 2020

It's a sorrowful new day on planet Earth.
Nearly one million people have died of COVID.

Grace is gone.
And RBG died today.
Love has fallen silent.
A friend of Mike and Cheryl's was killed last night while sleeping
    in bed—when during a storm outside of Atlanta, a tree fell
    on her house.
Dear God—WTF?

September 21, 2020

Some days America breaks my heart, makes me want to
Lift my allegiance and take it back.
Round the corners and cut out.
Head for the hills.
Hightail it to some other spot in the universe.

Fatefully embarrassed by the elevation of an ugly man
who came to power in America
and put everything of value at risk,
I weep over the wreckage of the past four years.
Are there enough life rafts for us to hop in and row away?
Enough new doors to open?
New vistas to lean into?
When panicking, will there be enough caring arms to wrap
around our frailty and reassure us of a better day coming?

Tissue is in short supply and still we weep.
Once casually draped scarves turn to shreds,
cut into masks and sizable hankies not to be shared
in the world of COVID.

If all the brokenhearted just sit down, sit down, and say, No!
No, you can't have it your way. No! You're just too mean.
What if we just sit down now?
We've been practicing for months, calling it "working from
    home."
But what if we really do sit down, just stop, and say,
No, you will not break my heart, not my country!

September 22, 2020

There isn't a single right answer, only the results produced.
I can choose what's right for me, I'm told.
I have free will.
I've exercised it, tried to make my will strong enough to bend
    things my way.
I hit a wall and named it Disappointment.
I turned away, seeking beauty.
Emboldened, my strong will floods me and again I reach for
    what is good.
Again, I have met the wall, full force.
Tears turn to fears and hope falls through the cracks.
I howl and listen quietly for a pack to shelter with.
As free will circles the drain, there must be those still standing
    who can lend a hand.
We can't all go down at once thinking there is no right answer.
Whose hand will you take?
And who will notice if it's blue or red, black or brown, white or
    gloved?

September 23, 2020

I was surprised to remember that I had failed to call.

I meant to, but day after day, I remembered that again I had failed to call.

Their outreach was well intended, but my heart was closed.

Growing smaller day by day requires less and less and allows so little to penetrate a bleak heart.

Too dark, too encapsulated in the pain of the world, I squinted into the sun and wondered how anything could ever be free again.

Can there be choices kindly expressed with good in mind?

Can people march peacefully with anger on display and not be beaten and killed?

Can it be safe to love and not fear loss?

Can one feel energized by life after sinking into the darkness this deep?

Some people break down in the darkness, that haunting, dark night of the soul.

Others, in the breaking down, reinvent themselves.

Will I be phoenix or ash?

October 3, 2020

Being of Norwegian ancestry has always seemed rather solid, the rarely recognized, stoic part of me aligned with strong and sober women who make great cookies with lots of butter. A peaceful northern tribe, hardworking, and with great tolerance for cold, gray weather.

This morning I'm pausing for a brief moment with my ancestors as Trump infects one more hallowed institution. Yesterday, I learned that a Norwegian diplomat has for the second time nominated Trump for the Nobel Peace Prize, and I am thinking critically about something I have held in high esteem throughout my life.

Since I was a child, I believed like most people that the Nobel Peace Prize recognized a person of value, valor, and contribution. The prize meant someone had done something miraculous, kind, and brilliant that would bless and benefit the world by bringing peace. But not today. Today, the nomination represents another loss in the respectful order of things pre-Trump, and I can't help but wonder how my Norwegian compatriot got it so wrong.

October 4, 2020

My concern today is for those whose encampment was bulldozed last week. Where are they now, these people I delivered food to after work? I brought them leftovers from the opulent drug-rep lunches served in the office each noon. And when I spilled the Chinese food in the backseat of my car, these people who made their home under the freeway ran for wipes and towels to help me clean up the mess. Where have they gone? Where is John? John, who introduced himself and with deep respect pointed out his brown tent and said if I ever needed anything I could find him there most of the time. Where is he now that the bulldozers have cleared another community of the unhoused and surrounded the area and remaining garbage with a tall black fence? Who will care for those who have so little?

December 7, 2020 (269 Days of Shelter-in-Place)
It's Surprising, Love

Have you too been surprised to find how working at home isolates you while opening your worried eyes to a greater purpose and desire? I make work the organizing activity of days that might otherwise lack meaning entirely. I'm surprised once again to find it dark outside when I quit work at the end of my day. I pour a glass of wine.

Have you too been surprised—when shopping once a month— how the most unusual things are attractive and wind up in the cart? Colorful, organic vegetables, too many to eat before they rot. Breads—enough to fill the freezer but thawed too easily for daily consumption. Salmon that demands to be eaten today to capture its full freshness when you were really thinking pizza. Meat—so beautifully arranged and clean in the case at Whole Foods, reminiscent of the meat you bought in 1985 in between vegetarian stints and when you had a family of four and a vibrant smile.

A pork roast became the focus of an entire Sunday afternoon recently while clipping herbs from the garden to chop and stuff it, admire, and bake it. I prepared that pork roast with joy, sweet potatoes, and artichokes on the side, and we had a retro Sunday supper. The flavor was familiar, but I didn't really like it. I'm glad Bryan did. I wrapped up the roast and sent it home with him. I offered a few suggestions for leftovers which he didn't need or want but accepted with a laugh and a "Thanks, Ma."

Have you too been surprised that this new round of stay-at-home edicts is hitting hard?

Like we tried it out, lived in absentia for nine months, did pretty
     well—
at least managed to stay alive and gain ten pounds.
It's winter now and dark and COVID seems a permanent life re-
     placement.
I want to run like hell
Into the fields of past mental freedom,
Out to swim with a whale.
Outside, six feet away with masked neighbors for friends,
I refuse the longing of my soul.
I watch whales on TV and channel surf.
And now it's almost Christmastime.
Are you too surprised?

Trump lost the 2020 election but claimed he won. We hardly had
a moment to celebrate, his insanity and followers so alarming in
the aftermath.

    And then, one of those every-now-and-then old boyfriends
called one cool November evening. We had unsuccessfully rekindled in the past, but these are vulnerable, lonely times and I
relented on my last never-again with him, just in case we might
have a different outlook—or outcome.

A Maybe-This-Time Love

Out of the blue, you called, wanting things to be different, "a
     better man" this time, you said.
Such a sorry pattern for me to fall for.

Playing at the edges once more, we rekindled our more-off-
than-on, twenty-five-year relationship.
It's COVID and I couldn't resist the spark of joy I felt.

I wanted to lean my body right up against your optimism until
you penetrated my every fear.
I wanted to construct a bridge between our shores of smooth
sand and rough edges, using tools newly crafted by your so-
briety and the pureness of your intention, and my natural
inclination to love and see beauty before it's fully evident.
I held in reserve my last never-again decision about you and let
my laughter spill out loud.
Because here you are again and it's COVID.

I wanted to tell you the truths of my heart and trust you to listen, understanding there is nothing to be fixed.
I wanted to look at your face and smile and believe you loved
me still after all these years, this older woman with the body
that no longer dances in lingerie for you on cool nights, your
boat swaying to the music with us.
I wanted to feel like myself again. Alive and light.

You shared your understanding of this insane world through
stories that brought me laughter and tears.
You entertained me with exquisite journeys into science, sea,
and space.
I loved your mind but you excluded my spirit.
The "love of your life," you said.
Yet so little of me felt included.

I tried to be more generous with my time and to silence my lurk-
ing "maybe."
But you took all the air and I began to feel lightheaded as you
filled my email inbox with your family photos and pictures of
you as a young man.
I didn't need your past. I needed a present strategy to survive
this hate-filled world.

You sent a hurt and brusque, emailed "goodbye," requesting I
not respond.
I wasn't committed, just interested and willing to see if maybe
this time we could find our way.
You have been a constant planet of possibility, a star in the
clouds, orbiting.
I'll keep my shades on and walk without looking up at you again.
Goodbye to you too.

348 days of Shelter-in-Place
The Mind Loves to Wander

I woke up this morning and became aware of my life, the one I
am living now with time to ponder!

My hazy morning eyes stopped at a print on the wall of my
bedroom. A large Michael Leu nude entitled *The Patio*, purchased
at the Fillmore Jazz Festival, a much anticipated and lively annual
event where I found many beautiful art pieces for my home and
body.

A feng shui master I once hired said I should get rid of the Michael Leu print. "Lovely, if you want to attract a woman, but if you want to attract a man, it should go!" I put away the source of feminine energetics as instructed, but when the man I was supposed to attract didn't show up and I grew bored with the feng shui redesign, I took my beloved print back from the garage and I love her still. I imagine she is me in the garden with wine, a book, and my relaxed lingerie falling off one shoulder and exposing a breast. Such deep inner peace in her body. So . . . as a friend once said to me when I added my two cents about the table narrowing the entrance at her front door, "Fuck feng shui!"

I picked up my buzzing phone to a news alert. This happens less frequently now that the ugly man is no longer president. His departure is such a relief after the trauma of the last four years and CNN alerting me of his minute-by-minute insults to the world. But today, seeing the word "trump" used as a verb in a sentence, I startled. How fragile is my recovery?

I am thinking about my life as a professional problem-solver. It's what I do: provide solutions to all kinds of problems for all kinds of people. But I am retiring. Sometimes, we choose a problem to work on and sometimes a problem chooses us. Despite appearances, I don't think the arrival of problems is all that random. I am restructuring now, without a business card or a problem to solve. I am learning to say the word "retired" and easing my way into a deeper inquiry about what I love.

I'm living a creative workshop of my own making.

I'll Find My Way

I retired. It ended with a sick and empty feeling in my stomach.

Retiring during COVID made for a lonely sendoff, despite a few
    cards, a couple of texts, a plant from one doctor, and a bottle
    of champagne from the two who couldn't wait for my job.

Six weeks later, I'm still lost in the sense that I must maximize
    the benefits of this strange time where nothing is required,
    short of hanging onto my sanity and finding the new path
    forward.

Ideas dance all around saying, "Do this, do that."

Critical indicators that I should be doing something that I'm not.

I will find my way once I've repotted the lemon tree.

After roses and trumpet vines cover the fence and my neigh-
    bor's lingering shadow.

Once I've chosen a diet of joy and lost the COVID weight I've
    gained this year.

You don't have to be Zen to get through this.

Just turn off the TV and face the sun.

Release

Retire—a word rooted in a foreign language that introduces a
    new reality lacking concept or container.

I am no longer the problem-solver and creative for the demands
    and desires of others.

I no longer have that one place to go where I am expected every
    day, that one place where if I didn't show up, someone
    would notice and follow up. The place where parts of me
    were known and accepted. The place where I gave myself

permission to experience myself in relationships and share my vulnerabilities and authenticity. The place where I understood my worth and continued to grow through the daily challenges.

I am now my own creative spirit exploring how delicious it feels to sleep until I wake up on my own time, without the jolt of an alarm and the immediate demands of the day.

"Choose love," the voice said so many years ago.

I agreed. I have been unfaithful at times. I listen for more.

She is more specific this time.

"Release your devotion to working hard and managing what is no longer yours.

Fall into your heart's desire and awaken to the artist who has been waiting.

It's easier than you think."

What Wisdom Could Come from Sleeping in the Sun?

The soft yellow carpet, warm in the afternoon sun.
Plush pillows and a comforter lounge on the daybed.
Open window and gentle blue curtains welcome the spring breeze.
Wind chime mirrors and tiny bells flicker and twirl with the light.
House plants perk up and stretch their leafy tips.
Book and waterglass, tea with lemon,
Notebook and pen, all within reach.
Wisdom is not guaranteed
but I am prepared for its arrival
while I nap in the warm, afternoon sun.

To Live Without Apology

Without apology I breathe
without apology I swallow
without apology I sing and I cry
and flood the flowers till their color pales.

Without apology I move through ponds and parks.
I dance a step with a bird and run from a bee without apology.
I speak without apology for truth that demands my voice
and I listen to old records with sorrow that not enough has
changed since 1972 when Marvin Gaye asked, "What's Goin'
On?" Still relevant, without apology.

Without apology I throw my arms carelessly into the air
and brush the empty nest into the river where it dissolves
into the natural occurrence of things long forgotten.
I move in my head through a lifetime of worry and uncertainty,
change and anxiety and unapologetically wish for more, for better.
I sing softly to this world that needs more peace and love, more
hope and joy.
I am unapologetically a vehicle for deeper understanding, and it
is unapologetically painful at times.

Let Them Say

Let them say I was frivolous, reckless, and selfish until they real-
    ized I was surviving the tremors of life in the time of
    COVID.

Let them say I cared. And then pulled myself up to a level of
self-care, which allowed me to be more effective. Less sym-
pathetic, perhaps.

Let them say I almost drowned in my tears before I hopped on a
log, turned it into a boat, and rowed to higher ground.

Let them say I appeared to know what I was doing, even in the
midst of such sorrow and uncertainty. And that I rebalanced
and carried on with love, leaving behind what I thought I knew.

Let them say I died to myself over and over, then rose up to
face the sun, shoulders back, chest high. And kept walking
into the woods, into the darkness that we live in now.

Let them say I changed: changed my plans, changed my mind,
loved and then didn't, opened and then shut.

Let them say I believed that God and the angels surrounded me.
Then sank alone into despair and uncertainty while smoke
billowed, choking states and countries miles away.

Let them say I was angry too. Focused on all that appears to
need change. But too undisciplined to do anything about it.
Paralyzed by the pain of the world.

Let them say I was living the best, most authentic life I could
figure out, day by day.

Let them say whatever the fuck they want. I will continue on,
my way.

And the Days Go By, Love
September 2021

Shock waves, one after another, limbering me up to revisit death
and the dance of life in her arms. September was a beast—worth
giving a little extra time to, throwing some love over the days

blurring into October. It's still warm on the patio, even at the beach, but this September called for a heavy blanket and good red wine. Of note:

1. GB's birthday, September 9—thirty-three years gone, but those of us who knew him still raise a glass in gratitude. His love changed my life. I am a braver, stronger person because he loved me.

2. One year since the death of my dear friend Grace and fearless phenom Ruth Bader Ginsberg—two powerful women whose legacies live on to inspire.

3. Holly and I survived a car crash that could have ended our lives but didn't. Left to live, what will I do with the balance of history and this open window to the future? I am alive and available to encounter the next noticeable moment of beauty and the next opportunity to grieve.

4. My brother Robert died eleven days ago. The minute-by-minute shock waves have subsided. Now I wake to a gentler realization of his transition. I feel less frantic as I wait for him to visit, wait for him to tell me all about heaven, wait for him to confirm our spiritual musings and the family conversations we've long anticipated would take place on the other side of time where love, truth, and service to all would be revealed.

5. The chiropractor cracks my body, releasing fear and pain with loud grunts of resistance. The fatigue that follows is not relieved by resting, but it's all I can do.

6. I've delayed returning phone calls, unable to chat or care too much. Briefly disconnected from the global sorrow, I take my time.

7. I go for a walk—one foot forward, then another. Such a simple reckoning with grief.

ACT VIII

Too Much for the Mind

Grief is too much for the mind, too controlling, too demanding.
So move it.
Allow it to float to parts unknown.
Into space above the clouds, where the view is beyond your
    earthly imagination.
Into treetops, where birds congregate and sing their uninhibited
    songs.
Allow grief to dive through the crushing waves,
    face down into the turbulent sand and let the salty water
    soothe and remind you of your healing capacity and wisdom.

Send grief to the labyrinth, carefully laid with rocks and crystals,
    embellished by creatures, feathers, and ferns.
Adorn your grief with tenderness, with love, with your affection.
Recognize when a gift is given and pick it up.
Tuck the feather in your hair and walk on.

Grief is too much for the mind,
So move it. Set it free.
Release it to the wind to fly to far-off places
    to find peace and expand into joy.
Feel your liberated mind in nature.
Go back, again and again
    until it is your most natural home.

For You, My Sisters, I Weep—Marilyn and Andee

We weep over the sheer beauty we witnessed together as we traversed life through our sisterhood for over fifty years. The joy of lush, fragrant jasmine in full bloom, the fluffy pampas grass on the scenic coastal roads we traveled a million times, the magnificence of the waves at the beach, and the exhilaration of a fast ride in an orange Mustang, Sissy-Lu specials filling our traveling goblets. The extravagance of our friendship filling our hearts.

Now, gone in mind or body or both, we weep. We weep over things forgotten on the way to the kitchen, and friends gone on; gone on to places we don't know or can't bear to imagine.

We weep over your strokes, those big and tiny, too many no matter their size. Arterial pathways to the brain closed unexpectedly, seizing the words you were desperate to speak, leaving you heartbroken, struggling to capture your thought before giving up and letting go with a frustrated huff and, "Oh, never mind."

We weep over the fall. Over the way your bones shattered and left you in agony, immobile and cold on the carpeted floor, thinly overlaying the concrete beneath. Lost and uncertain, angry and pale, wanting to walk freely into the shower and simply wash your hair, alone. Then Alzheimer's tapped you on the shoulder, becoming the next bridge to cross. You want to make your own decisions about how you will live, but that ability is slipping away faster than many realize. And now I weep because you don't want to talk about it anymore and I don't know what else to do.

I weep when the phone rings and I say hello and all I hear is your blaring television. Again, I am reminded that you can't hear or remember how to use the phone or TV, and you don't know that you've called me five times already this morning but have yet to say hello.

I want to wake up to a new day that includes mended bones, minds restored, and big rings slapping the table for emphasis. I want to see your bright smiles flashing, radiating the love you're known for. I want to talk over what's on our hearts and minds. I want us to be us again.

But everything has changed. Because today among the three of us, I alone can get up and walk to the kitchen for coffee and enjoy cooking breakfast. I alone can do what is necessary. I should be grateful, but I miss you, my sisters, and I weep.

You have left me and my place of belonging in the family of our creation,
leaving me to count my blessings and the imperfections of love and life without you.
Sadly, I must accept my fate.
And give myself permission to be a happy woman loving my life just as it is.

Love Dips

The sky is gray again. Smoke hangs below the clouds and hides
   the blue from sight. The birds are quiet. I wonder where they
   hide, where they find a tiny breath when the entire sky is
   covered in smoke? It's fire season again, previously known as
   "summer."
This morning, a tall, dry tree is being removed from the yard
   across the street. It's a terrible sound of sawing, then silence,
   more sawing, then a crack as large branches fall to the
   ground into a heap—a pile to be chopped into sawdust or
   garden mulch. Is this act of destruction prevention, or a sad
   response to fear?
The sky is smoke-filled, the tree branches have turned to kin-
   dling, and our politics are more fragile and violent than ever.

Afghanistan is falling and her people are scared witless, running,
   hanging on to the bodies of planes determined to fly away
   without them.
Her people who dangle from wings and tires will be left behind,
   their lives and hopes splattered on the tarmac.

This America frightens me.
But many still risk their lives to get here—
Only to encounter our inhumane reception.
How great must their fear be?
Is there really something worth fighting for? Worth dying for?

My friends and family are aging, some more gracefully than others.
Some under the threat of advancing diseases of body and mind.

Dementia and Alzheimer's unbearable to witness and harder to
    care for
Leaving me alone, exhausted, and heartbroken.

Is there anything worth living for? I ask.
Who is keeping the dream alive?
Again and again, the empath sinks, broken by the weight of pain
    magnetizing her to the deep, collective sorrow. With inten-
    tion, I command myself to pull up from the magnetic field of
    the empath, to rise above that level of collective pain so
    prevalent in the world. I am alive, and therefore here to be of
    good use.

Aging

The willow tree bends gracefully to the ground
without a care.
Tiny green leaves shimmer in the sun
and glittering beams slip between,
casting shadows.
There is an unspoken elegance to willow trees
and women who grow old without hesitance.

Thinking Love Over

We begin our journey of self-discovery in our family of birth,
being the tiniest doll at the center of the universe—if only for a
moment. As little children, Holly and Bryan got showered with
love and attention: two parents thrilled with their arrival,

nurturing the desire to tend to their little baby hearts, provide love, a home and safety, and the joy of growing up in a house of fun, laughter, honesty, and space for their feelings and ideas. I wanted them to know beauty and books, music, sports, theater, and art. They remember those days clearly. Mostly, I wanted them to feel safe and loved and have the life skills I anticipated they would need. I wanted to protect them from racism and hate and infuse them with everything I had learned in the hope of saving them from pain and sorrow, but all my efforts couldn't spare them. A bitter lesson, that one. But they know me as brave and smart and fierce in my love for them—they will always know that.

Like those little Russian nesting dolls, our memories secret away in former versions of ourselves: wife, mother, sister, daughter, friend, professional, student, success, failure. The list goes on, depending on how much we've put into living. Roles that we nurtured and integrated over time, roles that right here, right now can only be glimpsed in vignettes and photographs, mostly more beautiful as hindsight allows their softer sides to shine. As wife to three disparate men, I too was different. Each man brought out different qualities within me and the opportunity to explore my nature in relation to theirs. This was the case with men I dated, danced, romanced, and lived with and without. I'm grateful for each one who crossed my path. No matter their significance or steadfastness along the path of my life, I grew.

When you love a lot of people, you lose a lot of people. Over the course of a lifetime, you grow apart, you have a change of mind, a change of heart. What once fit no longer does. You adventure off in different directions, sometimes for no reason having nothing to do with the relationship—and sometimes, for every reason having to do with the relationship. And at some point in our humanness, we die.

In the soft light of morning, the outdoor sounds—rustling leaves and birds waking to sing morning into being—extract what feels like the best of me. A fifteen-minute walk to the neighborhood rose garden makes me happy. A joyful resting place for my spirit. Rejuvenated, I reach out to tug a thornless stretch of stem toward me. I smell the roses and walk home.

Is this the life I dreamt of when I still had the courage to dream? Could be.

A Little of Love's Healing Wisdom Came My Way

I watched a bird, a little chickadee, build a nest and care for her single egg in the camellia bush outside my kitchen window a few weeks ago. She would return from a brief flight for food most mornings at about nine-thirty. One morning last week, she landed as usual and hopped into her nest. Then, she hopped out and began jumping chaotically from branch to branch, then, back to her nest. Next, she became still, just looking around until she knew. It was then that I knew too. Her nest was empty. While unattended, a cat, or possibly a larger bird, had raided her nest. I saw her confusion and I watched as she came to terms with her new reality. Eventually, she flew away and has not returned. I swept up the remnants her marauder left on the ground. Only her empty nest remains in the camellia outside my window. And now, each morning, I think, *Nature—that is the nature of things*.

I grew a slender pink-and-purple sunflower for my brother Robert. He loved sunflowers. His birthday is coming up, his first since he died ten months ago. Yesterday, I went to say good morning and photograph the progressive beauty I'd been enjoying, but the flower was gone. Snapped at the stem and hauled away without a trace of a petal. "Goddamn squirrels!" I cursed. And then, I thought, *Nature—that is the nature of things.*

At what point do we accept the nature of things? When we have no choice but to adjust to an empty nest? When we must acknowledge that the sunflower blossom is gone? When we must change from lover to caregiver, not yet realizing it's all the same love? When our beloved dies?

Perhaps acceptance happens when we release our judgment about the past. It is easy to judge the marauder that robbed the chickadee nest or the pest that stole the sunflower. What is harder is trying to accept a new reality without self-judgment or judgment of others. Judgement is a natural human instinct, born of survival, but being judged can be painful, and to be the one judging and struggling to be right is also challenging. Judgment often seems inexplicable and uncomfortable and therefore goes unexplained and unexplored, left to rot. It's the nature of judgment.

One opportunity to learn acceptance and release judgment is by embracing the lesson taught by the Zen master. While holding his goblet, the master explains to his students, "This glass is already broken," its eventual shattering inevitable, just as our bodies are already dying the moment we are born. The story teaches us the impermanence of all things, which then allows us to embrace the time we have to love fully, understanding that change is inevitable. The glass will break, and death is assured at some point. It's nature.

Courage will swell, and we will love our life.

It's our nature.

On the War in Ukraine—Day Eleven

Take only what you love. Anything else must be too much to
carry.

Take your children, your pets, your mother and father, your
wife, and your husband—only if he is too old to fight. I
don't know how to write about war.

Bundle your smallest treasures into shopping sacks and wheel-
aboard bags purchased to carry just a few things for a romantic weekend, or an overnight with friends; not your life
packed up in a rush to unpromised safety. What about food,
water, soap, COVID masks, a towel and toothbrush—with
your two arms full and the wheels falling off your bag while
crossing bombed-out bridges, how long will you be able to
hold on to what you love? How long before the unknown
will force you to choose again? You've already left your
home, your country. Only your beating heart and will to live
pushes you toward more uncertainty.

I don't know how to write about war, the one that is now eleven
days old or perhaps centuries—the one that rages inside me
or on the other side of time, for now on the other side of the
world. But it's coming and the impact is already being felt;
we will fight about that too.

The war inside wakes me in the night, questions my relationships
and how much wine I drank before bed, so happy to have the
company of a neighbor and a pot of soup with tangerines to share.
The war in the streets of Oakland where color and money separate us and guns are recklessly pointed and triggers pulled, bodies
of boys and girls, men and women blown into pieces the size of
the shooter's shattered hopes. This war too keeps me awake.

I don't know how to write about war, so I search for some wisdom of the ages where I find poems fallen from pens dipped in courage, sorrow, and fear, where mean-spirited and evil politicians pointed their fingers toward hell—even then.

I don't know how to write about war, but again I am eating it for breakfast, lunch, and dinner in living color, embarrassed by my comfort and freedom to change the channel, to walk outside, to pick up the hose, pluck a shriveled leaf, and sit down to admire the view and feel the warmth of the sun on my face. Such grace and gratitude hovers in unbearable contrast.

When hell freezes over and the blankets are passed around, the quiet will surely be terrifying.

To Holly and Bryan—My Forever-Loves

What I've been trying to tell you is about love.
So why does it sound like heartache and grief?
What is it about rainbows and wedding dresses that escapes me?
Why the flowers grow dry, and popsicles melt
    and there seems to be no hope
    that dreams do come true.
Too much sadness is all around and too much anger.
And yet—the sun is stunning, and I have coffee and pajamas
    and memories.
I want to tell you about love. The kind that lives forever.
Deeply influencing love, even today.
I want to tell you how I love the way you walk, the way you
    smile.
I want to tell you how you made me smile when little else could.

I want to tell you that tomorrow will always be better, (but you already know that isn't true).

But know this—sometimes, when we open to the space beyond fear and wipe away our tears, we can be amazed.

We can't force these moments or fantasize them, visualize, wish, or pray them into being. They just come.

And when they do, it's best to notice.

Remember the moments when you feel good, the moments you feel joy.

Let them build a memory; create a muscle that will strengthen you in times of stress, deep despair, and loss.

Loss is part of the heart math that multiplies, adds, divides, and subtracts the grief of our growth. The math is always keeping track, recording our part in Life, our stiches in the Divine Tapestry.

In the end, it's our experience and how we saw it.

Like photographing our moments of good and sorrow, pleasure and pain.

A million smiles and a million tears and here we are.

Either way, resilience is essential.

Compassion makes you a better person.

Love insists on being present.

Find peace.

Find your people.

Express your concerns and your caring.

Try to find more reasons to smile than to cry.

If the math doesn't work out that way,

may some of your tears be joyful.

Choose Love

The tendency to be done, move on, burn it down, blow it up, rebuild, and find a way has been in me for as long as I can remember. I was blessed with tenacity and an optimistic spirit whose limits have been tested. I grew up believing the fairy tales that always included true love and a happy ending. I hoped that beauty and love were the ultimate gifts we could all expect . . . if we were good. And I tried to be good.

In this life we plan, we look ahead, and to the extent of our interest and energy, capacity and creativity, we do what we think we should or think will fulfill our needs—and then life happens. And still, we work hard, and we try to be good. With all that, it is stunning to realize that we never really know what's coming. We do our best. But life guarantees no happy ending.

There are happy moments: the moment before deciding to burn my journals, perhaps, when the promise of new love with Frank had given me courage to believe. Or the moment the angel's voice called my name, waking me in the middle of the night, tenderly, repeating, "Choose love. Choose love." Or the happy moment some years earlier when I came home from shopping with a sexy, strapless, black velvet dress, perfect for the Caribbean cruise GB and I had been planning for months over dinners with three other couples, just two weeks before the cancer diagnosis that led to his first surgery on the day the ship sailed. We never know what's coming. And now, I consider a happy ending might be going to sleep one night and not waking up, rather than a nasty diagnosis that kicks my ass right to the finish line. But I'm in no rush!

The main constant throughout my life has been my desire to understand, to develop context as a way of making sense of what comes, and to survive with some measure of grace. This is a story of commitment and determination. The living of it has been rich: grief- and joy-filled, fun, depressing, painful, beautiful, interesting, spiritual, loving, awakening, and meaningful. The writing of it has called me deeper and in the end I'm simply grateful.

This is a love story about the most elusive and profound love I know, the love I have worked hardest to achieve. It is the story of my journey to love my life, even without the happy ending. It continues to be a work in progress.

I am connected to the sea.
I rub stones and create sand
that can blow in the wind
and build mountains.
I am strong, capable, unmoved by your judgment.
Reaching beyond my own, I seek liberation, even now.
I choose love.

Soul Resonance Love Map

When the fairytales died, and the truth of life took hold,
I created some worthy distractions that supported my desire to
    live a life I loved.
I sheltered among friends and created a family I loved in the ab-
    sence of the one into which I was born.
I read and studied and expanded my awareness and understanding.
I nurtured my heart and followed my mission to choose love.
I grew beyond the years when before daylight I was barely able
    to delay a call to apologize for myself—a word or response
    that spontaneously escaped and could have exposed my pain.

Times when, like me, the recipient of my call was typically
focused on the hurt or discomfort I had caused them.

I recognize the global pain that has become personal and lives in
my body. With this, I cultivate compassion.

I vote against the Trump agenda and attend to my constant fear
of the hatred he has generated and encouraged to roam free.

Many days I wake up to find my heart broken, tears filling my
eyes before the light shines through.

The murderous use of guns by the insane and the angry, the
pained and the privileged.

The lives of children threatened while in school and the stress of
enduring real time newsfeeds from the moment they are old
enough to translate the terror in their parents' eyes.

The oppression and abuse of women, the murder and villainiza-
tion of Black men, the destruction of communities, and the
harassment and threat to those judged as other or different.

The lesser-caring minds that allow it all to continue.

I wake and my heart is broken some days.

I welcome joy whenever it shows up.

I allow beauty and nature to comfort and inspire me.

I think about dying. I think about others dying. I read somewhere that it is good to think about dying at least three times
a day. I do. I have since I was thirteen.

I have been uncomfortable in this life. I have grown through the
honesty of my despair.

My soul still longs for deep connection,

Another sunny day and hands to hold.

Some days, that's exactly what shows up

And I am grateful for another happy moment.

Another day to choose love.

Another day to choose to love my life.

Afterword

Dear Reader,

This book blesses a serious girl who insisted that Love not be vanquished.

She built resilience with her intention to live fully, give from her heart, and align with her soul.

She persevered and loved herself into a more joyful woman, still serious, but with deep appreciation for changing hearts and minds, even when the happy ending eluded her.

There is a way forward
even at the end
of a poem,
of a story,
of a life.

Volumes have been written about misogyny, politics, war, racism, civil rights, and injustice. Though my story weaves through these larger forces, this book is personal. I am a seventy-five-year-old white woman who brought two biracial children into this unaccepting world. I did my best to educate my children about the realities of what is abhorrent and beyond understanding. To teach them that all of life is connected—no exceptions.

My life is a love story fueled by my heartfelt intention to grow, learn, and help others to recognize the best in themselves. Despite the losses I've endured, I am sustained by beauty, understanding, and the active desire to love my life. I believe my love has inspired my children to live generously, giving from their flow of love and promise. I hope that my readers will find a heartfelt connection to do the same.

May you be blessed and choose love.

—Meridian

Appreciations

To Linda Maree, the creative founder of Bee Write writing group in Sarasota, Florida, and the amazing women who gathered at the table in the tearoom at Selby Gardens each week to write and share a safe and supportive space. You heard my first spontaneously written words spoken out loud. Your encouragement helped me to consider the possibility of my own creative voice being shared. Thank you.

To Marika and John, Cindy and Roy, who so honored how much I missed my writing group in Sarasota when I moved home to Oakland: Thank you for playing with me and turning dessert at our Saturday night wine dinners into boisterously delicious writing time that so honored our stories calling to be told and the creative potential within us. It deepened our friendships and took us each to a new level of expression. Here's to the Wine Writers!

Thanks to Terri Tate, who welcomed the Wine Writers into her writing group and opened a Zoom space to keep us together through COVID. It kept us connected, butts in chairs, writing! I am grateful for your support Terri and for each one who showed up to share, read, and critique each week.

To Laurie Wagner and the Wild Writing Family, my deep appreciation, love and respect. Introduced to Wild Writing in 2017, I began the practice. This was my refuge when COVID and politics slammed our lives. Thank you for modelling such honest presence and for holding sacred space so profoundly that I made it through those troubling times, holding the thread of your video message and poetry three times each week. With your encouragement to write "knowing we already love you," I wrote this book.

Gratitude always to The Narrative Project: to Cami Ostman for creating this program and being a seemingly tireless, always engaging teacher at the weekend seminars and online. The content development of the program is excellent and the writers it attracts are a talented reflection. Thanks also for the introduction to publisher Lisa Dailey, who I am just starting to work with.

Thanks to Annaleise Kamola, who was my first contact and intake interviewer. You are the reason I chose this program. You met me exactly where I was (a mess at that particular moment, as I recall!) and guided me through the development arc of this book with skill, grace, and wisdom beyond your earthly years. Your depth of connection is what I crave in this life.

To Devon Fredericksen, my coach and critique group leader, who became my very solid and instructive developmental editor: Thank you for your elegance as a writer, a critic, a coach, and a human. You held my work tenderly and convinced me that there was validity and value in sharing the poetry of my story.

To Carol, Lora, and Lisa, my critique group, heartfelt thanks. It was a privilege to read your work. Your contributions to mine prompted new levels of thought and consideration. I'm grateful to have shared our time and dedication through this amazing process. Write on friends!

To Dana, Vanessa, and Erin, thank you for adopting me into your group during the weekend retreats; I'm so grateful. Our time on the road between Bellingham and Seattle, trips to Trader Joe's, the lunches and dinners we shared, and most especially the conversation and generosity of getting to know you made those weekends for me. Ultimately, it was my relationship with Dana that nurtured this book into existence.

To my first beta reader, Erin Curlett, I treasure the time you carved out of your magnificently focused, demanding, and loving life. The depth of insight you offered and the love you extended was invaluable.

To everyone else I connected with through TNP, thank you. It was a wonderful experience and I'm happy to have spent time with you in the container of our shared hopes and dreams and willingness to do the work. You're awesome and I can't wait to read your books!

To Dana Tye Rally, copyeditor extraordinaire, I can't imagine I would have made it through editing with anyone but you. Your skill and knowledge, your attention to detail, and your commitment to the work is phenomenal. But it's your heart and spirit of generosity that got this book and my backslides into uncertainty, my moments of gut-wrenching loss of confidence and fear of being so vulnerable, over the finish line. I am forever grateful and will hold you, your friendship, and your family in love always.

To my dear friends Dolores, Marika, and Cindy, who were my first-version beta readers and ongoing consultants: Each one of you gave me your ideas, love, support, wisdom, and insight into me and the various issues included in this book. You gave from your heart every step of the way. Thank you always for your authenticity and intention to love your lives with truth, depth, and integrity.

To my spirit sister Sharie: Thank you for your love, support, and your contributions to the memories of our journeys together during Three of Hearts and ever after. Special thanks for being a powerful survivor, holding strong, and for introducing me to Wild Writing!

To Howard: Thanks for always seeing the glass half full. I see more wine tasting in our future.

To Marilyn, who swore she was going to buy the first copy. Rest in peace, my sister.

To Marina, Millie, and Ellia, welcome to the family of my heart. I love you and the grandma you inspired in me. That part has brought me to life in a whole new way and I love being your Mama Meridian.

To the many friends and family not mentioned by name, with love, I thank you. Your presence on this journey has kept me committed to the exploration of life and love.

Finally, to my beloveds, Holly and Bryan. You have been my reason for everything. I love you.

About the Author

Meridian Kristi is a poet who writes about the quiet, often-overlooked beauty amid the painful realities of her life in this uncertain world. Through words, she maps new pathways of healing and hope for those who have suffered unbearable loss. Kristi has spent her career contributing to the quality of care and management in the medical profession. She is the founder of Practice With CARE, a consulting and coaching service for health

Photo by Marina Almaraz

care professionals who choose to practice excellence and compassion. She also created Women 'Round the Table, where she led workshops to help women embrace their journey to courageously cultivate a life they love. From healthcare to leadership to interior design (Meridian Visions ~ Interiors Inspired by Love), Kristi is deeply attuned to the energetic and intuitive aspects of life that allow the heart and mind to work harmoniously. She holds a master's degree in health services administration and a bachelor's degree in holistic health. She lives in the Bay Area with her cat, Paris.

Printed in the USA
CPSIA information can be obtained
at www.ICGtesting.com
LVHW091320270924
792207LV00007B/651